Kinds of Blue

Another one for
"The Countess Cathleen"
from her admirer Wayne,
with a fond hello from
someone who wishes
you nothing but joy —

Al
Young
at the close
of
1984.

By Al Young

Fiction
SNAKES
WHO IS ANGELINA?
SITTING PRETTY
ASK ME NOW

Poetry
DANCING
THE SONG TURNING BACK INTO ITSELF
GEOGRAPHY OF THE NEAR PAST
THE BLUES DON'T CHANGE

Non-Fiction
BODIES & SOUL
KINDS OF BLUE

Editor
CALIFÍA: *The California Poetry* (with Ishmael Reed, *et al*)
YARDBIRD LIVES! (with Ishmael Reed)

Kinds of Blue

of

musical memoirs by

Al Young

DONALD S. ELLIS • PUBLISHER • SAN FRANCISCO

Creative Arts Book Company • 1984

Several of these selections, in different form or context, previously appeared in *Big Rock Candy Mountain, California Living, Jeopardy, Love, 19 New American Poets of the Golden Gate,* and Bonnie Lateiner's *Volition.*

"But Beautiful" was commissioned by Orrin Keepnews as liner notes for the Kenny Dorham album, *But Beautiful* (Prestige Records). The first half of "Breezin' " also happens to be the jacket copy for George Benson's Warner Bros. LP of the same title.

The material quoted in the Author's Note is from *The Mysticism of Sound; The Power of the Word; Cosmic Language:* The Sufi Message of Hazrat Inayat Khan (Copyright © 1962, 1973 and published by the International Headquarters of the Sufi Movement, Geneva).

Published by Donald S. Ellis, San Francisco
and distributed by
Creative Arts Book Company
833 Bancroft Way, Berkeley, California 94710
Printed in the United States of America

Typography: Green Valley Graphics

ISBN 0-916870-82-0
Library of Congress No. 84-70287

Cover illustration by Ronald Dahl

The publication of this book was made possible in part by a grant from the California Arts Council

CONTENTS

For Luciano and Rita Federighi, real friends.

AUTHOR'S NOTE

These are simply joyfully written pages conceived in the spirit of fun.

Like its companion volume, *Bodies & Soul,* this little book is intended to entertain readers and listeners everywhere and is aimed at no audience in particular. I have taken pain to try and translate the particularities of my own musical experience—in which American jazz and popular music figure prominently—into universal terms. A given selection can be about a specific piece of music, its performers, circumstances under which it first reached my consciousness, or the chord it struck in me and my life at the time. Occasionally I've made an effort to articulate the purely emotional or mental or spiritual effects of music in poetic terms. I know readers will erect their own worlds from the words set down here simply by letting the jeweled needles of their imagination transport them, line by line, through the grooves of these written records of my own comings and goings in the universes of music and sound.

It might sound a little crazy, put that way, but music, sound itself, is even crazier. What's to it? A few notes, a lot of silence, a beat or pulse, some harmonies, breath, muscle, bite, heart, the sigh of the spirit longing to express itself beyond the range of bodily confinement.

Sitting in the LP-walled music room at the home of my Italian translator, Luciano Federighi, in the heart of northern Italy, I find myself being whisked back to the Mississippi of my childhood when he puts on a record by J.B. Lenoir, another country blues genius who has left this plane of existence. How easily we shift from black rural sounds to the voice of Jo Stafford singing "Dancing in the Dark," or the melting voice and soprano saxophone of Pony Poindexter breathing new life into Miles Davis's "All Blues."

Or suddenly, weeks later, I'm back in Manhattan, locked inside a hot, fetid subway as it roars through tunneled darkness from Pennsylvania Station to West 14th Street. My ears, like the bones in my body, are rumbling and yet, across the aisle, there's a young man clutching his high-powered, twin-speakered AM/FM/Cassette radio, blasting Michael Jackson's "Thriller" and nodding in rhythm behind impenetrable, light-proof sunglasses.

And in lovely Spokane, at the home of poet James McAuley and his wife Deirdre, loquacious Dubliners, I ask what the sweet music is coming from the livingroom one morning at breakfast and, beaming, he gets up from the table and goes to bring me the tape of Korean soprano Kiri Te Kanawa singing Mozart Opera Arias with Sir Colin Davis conducting the London Symphony. I start thinking about Korea and Mozart and my visit to London back when punk rock was still an expression of youthful, workingclass rebellion, long before profit-conscious recording executives imported it to America, re-dubbed it New Wave and sold it to apolitical middleclass kids. I thought about the days in the paleolithic Fifties when a bunch of us Hutchins Intermediate School kids in Detroit—sometimes as many as ten at a time—would roam the streets, singing King Pleasure's "Moody's Mood for Love" at the top of our lungs for the express purpose of blowing grown folks and other squares away. And I thought about King Pleasure himself, Clarence Beek, a mystic who, according to singer-lyricist Jon Henricks, was last heard from in the Tibetan Himalayas where he'd gone to pursue at length the mystery of existence.

Perhaps it's the mystics who make the most sense when it comes to explaining the mystery and all-out appeal of music. "As to what we call music in everyday language," says Hazrat Inayat Khan, himself a vina player and one of India's greatest musicians, "to me architecture is music, gardening is music, farming is music, painting is music, poetry is music. In all the occupations of life where beauty has been an inspiration, where the divine wine has been poured out, there is music. But among all the different arts, the art of music has been specially considered divine, because it is the exact miniature of the law working through the whole universe. For instance, if we study ourselves we shall find that the beats of the pulse and the heart, the inhaling and exhaling of the breath, are all the work of rhythm. Life depends upon the rhythmic working of the whole mechanism of the body. Breath manifests as voice, as word, as sound; and the sound is continually audible, the sound without and the sound within ourselves. That is music; it shows that there is music both outside and within ourselves."

Now it's your turn to solo.

—Al Young,
Viareggio, Italy;
New York City and
Spokane, Washington,
1983-1984

Music, when soft voices die,
Vibrates in the memory.
> —Percy Bysshe Shelley

The sea, the sky
and you and I;
sea and sky
and you and I,
we're all blues.
All shades, all hues,
we're all blues.
> —Oscar Brown, Jr.
> (from his lyrics to
> Miles Davis's "All Blues")

JAVA JIVE

The Ink Spots, 1943

For several mornings at the age of three, I stood quietly by the livingroom window in our little one-story house in Ocean Springs and studied the way a spider trapped a fly in his web and carefully devoured her. Why I thought the fly was a she and the spider a he would be tough to explain, but that was the way it played in my literal head of dream pictures whose images, now that I think about it, were clearly made up of tiny quivering dots the way magazine or newspaper photos look when you subject them to intensive magnification.

Words didn't come easily for what I was seeing, yet somehow I knew deep beneath or beyond what little mind I must've had by then that I was glimpsing a mystery of some kind; some important, worldly essence was being vividly played out before my unblinking eyes.

Then, finally, it all fell into place. The sun—like a hot, luminous magnet—happened to be shining powerfully that antique afternoon. My father was busy being his auto mechanic self and I could see him through the dusty window-screen out there in the grass and dirt and clay of the sideyard driveway, fixing on our dark blue Chevy coupe, grease all over his face and forearms; black on black. Pious as a minister or metaphysician, he was bent on fixing that car.

My mother was in the next room, the kitchen, fixing redbeans and rice. My very intestines were tingling with gladness, for redbeans and rice, as far as I was concerned, had no parallel; there simply wasn't anything like it anywhere in the world, whatever the world was. To dine everyday on redbeans and rice—or to breakfast, lunch or snack on them—would've suited me just fine. Lifetimes from my spider-and-fly-moment, just before nightfall, I knew we children would be gobbling our portions of dinner— complete with chopped onions and oleomargarined slices of white Bond bread—on the linoleum down under the kitchen table with newspaper for placemats. And I'd be spoiling to tell everybody about the spider and how he'd stuck it to the fly with his web, even though it was going to be years—and I seem to have glimpsed this too—before I'd be able to make heads or tails of any of it, in words anyway.

From the big Zenith radio console, its wood case shining with furniture oil, probably lemon, the Ink Spots were singing "Java Jive." Except for "I like coffee/I like tea," the words made no sense to me, but I liked the way the tune kept winding around and around to make its point, and I loved the way they came out of it all with: "A cup/a cup/a cup/a cup/a cup, ahhhhhhh!" That sigh at the tag meant everything, said it all: it signalled my Aunt Ethel, the big coffee addict in the family who, even then, always came to mind with her lips cradling the edge of some hot cup, breathing and exhaling steam and steaminess; big fogs of warmth in which sugar and sweetmilk or Pet Milk played some part. Watching her I could not fail to get the idea that something glad was going on between Aunt Ethel and that coffee of hers. If you or anyone else had taken time out to explain that the coffee bean and its narcotizing effect on people everywhere was an industry that involved colored peoples doing the picking all over the world, I wouldn't have connected with what you were saying anymore than I would've understood the meaning of the Man in the Moon, but I might've had a notion. Around the same time, you see, the Andrews Sisters were drawing checks off something called "They've Got an Awful Lot of Coffee in Brazil."

Being three, you see, isn't that much different from being a hundred and three, particularly when you begin to understand it's all a matter of putting two and two together.

July seeped into the room, quiescent with harmony and heat, the beat; the beating of the fly's wings as the spider ingested her from head to toe; boodie and sole. I stood there. I stood still. Time stood still and the whole of Mississippi, maybe the whole world, stood there soaking up this three-year-old's vision of how the world really works whether you realize it or not. It was as if, for me at least at that moment, my father had pried open the engine of life itself and motioned me over to have a look at how it worked and then, without so much as a 7th grade shop class explanation, snapped the lid back on, leaving me with the idea that there was something, some mechanism or cause that lay behind any and everything I would ever experience in this ever-shifting, not-to-be-believed existence that mystics—when you boil what they say down to a simmering, low gravy—say is only a movie, the acting out of something vaster than ourselves; the cosmic drama, if you will.

I wanted to taste this java, sample this coffee, this tea they were rhythmizing so invitingly. Feeling my insides beginning to gladden, I rushed out into the yard to hear my father say, "Hey, Skippy! C'mere, boy, and gimme some sugar!"—meaning: *Let me kiss you smack on the jaw.* I liked that. I liked it so much, I got confused. I wanted to race over and blurt out to him everything I'd just figured out about the spider and the world and the mystery and the tingling I felt inside, even though I didn't feel ready yet to pull the words together. There were no words, really; there was only this soundless understanding puffing up with feeling like a rainbow-colored balloon filling up all too fast with smooth summer air.

Just then, just as I was about to make my move toward Daddy, I saw a bright aquaplane zoom in close overhead, low enough for me to see the pilot, a white man, making me think at once of a crisp, airborne Nabisco saltine. He was wearing one of those oldtime aviator helmets with earflaps and goggles. He waved at me. He waved and smiled and now, millions of mind-hours later, I can draw a wayward cloud of a comic strip balloon over his head that shows him thinking: "Long as I'm up here foolin around, lemme just wave at that lil ole colored boy on the ground down there and give him a thrill!"

This bubbling moment and all that led up to it—like the family's first tentative move to Detroit and the unbelievable coldness of ice and snow and the tight light of what my folks kept calling "movin upnorth to the city"—is etched into me like the lines of some play; a kind of play that's had to settle for being sliced up over the years into what I eventually learned to call poetry or prose.

We lived close enough to the Gulf of Mexico for low-flying aquaplanes to be a commonplace, but that had been the very first time I'd ever seen a pilot up close. It was entirely different from those black-out nights when coastal air raid alerts were up, when Ella Mae Morse would be on the Zenith singing "The House of Blue Lights" and there we'd be, me and my brothers sprawled on the floor or blanketed down in bed, listening and remembering, with those blue emergency lightbulbs screwed into the lamp and ceiling sockets, their cooling glow softening the edge that was forever cutting a line between the seeable and the hearable worlds.

I rushed into my father's arms, gave him that sugar, wondering why we called those people crackers and why kids weren't supposed to fool with coffee.

As for the spider and the fly and my insights into the mystery of that spectacle, all I can say is that the craziness of

4

my excitement has thickened over the years. Now I'm given to believing that the web is only the world, the spider desire, and the fly the fickle, innocent and positively neutral nature of existence. Beyond that stands some youthful presence, more consciousness than thing, taking it all in with astonishment and, as a matter of fact, aiding and abetting and allowing it all to happen as if—like the web—it was either staged or created by design.

GREEN ONIONS
Booker T. & the MG's, 1962

"Dress the part," American humorist and realist George Ade used to say, "and the role plays itself." The dress was laboratory garb, which mostly meant a clean, crisply starched white lab coat. Whether you chose to wear a dress shirt or tie beneath it was strictly a personal matter, but everybody on the job, intentionally or not, eventually developed some kind of relationship with this uniform.

As for me, I was a lab aide, one of two at the Laboratory for Comparative Biology out in Richmond, California. Our job was to wash chemical glassware and other apparatus such as testubes, beakers, flasks, pipettes, crucibles, weighing bottles, and so forth. We were also responsible for the sterilization of certain articles and solutions, and this usually involved subjecting them to high temperatures in the autoclave. Washing was done in an acid bath solution and for this you wore heavy rubber gloves and a hooded mask. That acid solution was something else; the fumes alone slowly ate away your clothing and you had to be extra careful about rinsing all traces of it from your skin. I used to have nightmares about the stuff.

Lab aides were flunkies; the maintenance crew of the scientific world. You were the one they pulled over to assist in the preparation or analysis of experiments of any kind. One day you might find yourself running organic substances or samples through the centrifuge machine; another day you might be sitting at a table or bench, stringing or snapping green beans or chopping up the stems of green onions. It was a gig that was anything but dull, and I must say I never worked around so many lab-coated eccentrics as I did the year I spent at LCB which was housed in the lab wing of Kaiser Hospital in working class Richmond. Anything was likely to happen and usually did.

Booker T. and the MG's came out with "Green Onions" the year I started work there and it was always playing on the jukebox either at the A&W Root Beer franchise across the street, or at Gray's Club a little further down on Cutting Boulevard, or at the Slick Chick, a cryptic greasy spoon, along the same strip. There was also a chili joint whose name I've forgotten where I'd go for lunch with Ethel Holmes, the older black woman who was the other fulltime lab aide in this operation. We'd sit there—a Louisianan and a Mississippian—munching on our chili beans and rice, talking that drowsy stuff Southerners and ex-Southerners slip into whenever they get together, listening to Booker T. Jones, Steve Cropper and the rest of the MG's laying down that jumping, bluesy Memphis sound in the background.

"Green Onions" was on the radio, on the jukeboxes and, subliminally it seems, on everybody's mind. If you paid close attention—as I did at the time, for I was also gigging weekends in coffee houses and cabarets, singing and playing guitar—you could hear how this particular tune with its mesmerizing vamp was influencing pop music. You couldn't get away from "Green Onions," and the fact that it was an instrumental probably lengthened its life considerably. An elderly gentleman at a neighborhood house party told me, "How come it look like everything else seem to come and go, but people still crazy bout 'Green Onions'? You in the music business, so explain that to me if you can."

I couldn't explain it, but I did know it was infectious. The Gray's Club I speak of was about as elemental as they came. The sign out front was hand-lettered and semi-literate. The "S" in Gray's had been brushed on in such a way that it looked bigger than the rest of the name, and the letterer hadn't bothered painting in an apostrophe. Wes Jacobs, who was one of two black lab assistants at LCB, used to call it the Gray S Club, and that name stuck. Wes was a Buffaloan who, like me, had done time in Detroit and Ann Arbor. "Hey," he'd say, "they're throwin another one of those Blue Monday parties over at the Gray S Club. What say we jump in there and pick up on some of those free turnip greens and cornbread and blackeyed peas and fried chicken?" And that's what we'd do after work some Mondays. They'd be advertising blues singer Jimmy McCracklin, scheduled for Friday and Saturday night, but guess what they'd be playing on the jukebox?

Whenever I'd show up anyplace in my lab coat, and expecially if I wore a tie, which I did sometimes just to bolster the old ego or give my low status a momentary, arbitrary facelift, people behind the counters would often— usually after making change—say something like, "You know, Doctor, I been feelin this funny pain right up under my ribs for bout a week now. Like, when I breathe, that's when I feel it sharpest. What you reckon I oughtta do?"

At first, I'd trip all over myself trying to explain how I really wasn't a doctor and, look, you better have that checked out because it sounds serious to me. But after awhile, I came to realize it was the look of me, and only the look of me, they were responding to. That white lab coat was what rounded out the effect. Soon I'd change my tune, and when they'd hit me with their medical problems, I'd finger the pencil in my lab coat chest pocket, look away thoughtfully and say, "Take two aspirin, get a few good nights sleep, get some exercise and then tell me how you feel."

And, by Godfrey, it worked!

There was a fellow we'll call Janocz who'd come to the States from Hungary after the 1956 uprising by way of Brazil. Somewhere along the line, probably some moon-drenched night on a Rio beach, he'd got it in his head he was going to be a doctor of something. By the time he'd begun becoming an American citizen, he was working with one of the top biologists at LCB. One afternoon I happened to be present when the boss—a chunky woman, thoroughably lovable, with a round, Germanic face framed by a severe, short bowl-cut hairdo—asked Janocz to rattle off the valence of some chemical element. He, uh, he, uh, wasn't sure what she meant or, rather, what the valence should've been been, uh—That's when Janocz got busted down to the level of rat keeper for the resident toxicologist, an Austrian who, because he didn't hold a degree in medicine from an American school, had to travel the backroads and byways of the profession he'd been trained for. I remember he'd spent a lot of time on Tahiti and, at some point, had actually met the English novelist Somerset Maugham, or, rather—depending on which version of the story he was dishing out of a particular morning or afternoon—he had spent some time with the real-life woman who had served as the model for the prostitute become religious convert in Maugham's famous short story, "Rain." Joan Crawford portrayed her in *Sadie Thompson,* the movie based on that story. Either way, the good doctor was a voracious reader and lover of literature who was enamoured of the fact that Maugham, like himself, had been trained as a physician. He too had literary ambitions and planned some day to knock out a few short stories or maybe a novel or two about his own adventures and travels. For the time being, he was the LCB toxicologist—the Rat Man, we called him—and the one Dr. Allen farmed you out to assist when you started messing up and your lab future was growing uncertain.

I myself grew rather fast and loose in my handling of lab protocol as the months wore on, so that one reckless mid-morning Dr. Allen, brandishing her steely, businesslike grin, asked me to submit my schedule. That was the tip-off. When she asked you to submit a schedule—which was what she'd asked of Janocz—you could be certain you were skating on thin ice, indeed. Discipline around LCB, for lower level workers anyway, was anything but tight. With your hands pushed down into the pockets of your lab coat and, wearing the proper expression of authority, you could mingle leisurely and roam at large. Such roaming, if you didn't look out, was apt to get you in trouble.

I should perhaps explain that the facilities of the Laboratory for Comparative Biology were spread around the immediate neighborhood. The main facility, for example, was where my work was headquartered, but I had occasion— sometimes dozens of times a day—to walk across the street and make use of the autoclave, or to deliver specimens to the Rat Man or to pick up equipment that needed cleaning from any of several associates who ran mini-labs on that side of Cutting Boulevard. Further down the block was a storage and warehouse building. Another lab aide named Ken—one of two so named; both of them hired after Ethel and I had gotten on—used to go with me down there on one errand or another, and sometimes we'd linger and joke around for the fun of it. Or else Wes Jacobs and I would make a run over to Cutter Glass Labs or some other scientific firm along the Bay, on business, of course, and always with the blessings and under the unquestionable protection of our official uniforms.

It was Janocz, though, who took the cake when it came to abusing lab coat privileges. He actually had the nerve to wear his lab coat to work mornings, and he was fond of carrying a little black leather bag. Whenever Janocz got stopped for speeding by some highway patrolman, all he had to do was blush or look flustered, then point to his black bag on the car seat beside him and say, "Oh, officer, I must have gotten carried away in the face of this emergency." And the patrolman would inevitably presume him to be an M.D. of some kind and wave the little imposter on. Janocz was almost unstoppable. It took me a long time to catch on to his clever gambit of arriving late to the job, loosening his tie, then disappearing with a clipboard into one of the back rooms where he and his boss had some manner of experiment set up. That way, should Dr. Allen come looking for him, he could always emerge from his hideway, breathless and tousled, and give her the impression that he'd been on the scene all along, taking care of business.

At the time, I was in my early twenties. Everything was serious, but not too serious. A college dropout and would-be writer, I was busiest of all with life itself and the process of getting it lived. The idea here was to hold down enough of a day job to eat and meet the rent of $75 a month and to drop into a cookie jar the earnings I picked up from music gigs on the weekends and parttime disk-jockeying at a local radio station nights.

Along the way I gathered enough mental notes to paper a book on that lab experience which will always be punctuated with blasts from Booker T. & the MG's "Green Onions." Now I'm forced to realize that I was the one who was green at one end and sprouting at the other. And while shedding one layer after another, I was getting to know the world in ways that never paid off so much materially as they did experientially. It never occurred to me then, for instance, that there would have to be no fewer than a thousand chapters in this imagined volume devoted to that year, for the Laboratory for Comparative Biology—whose personnel came from the States, Europe, Japan, India, China, Canada, Australia, and the Middle East—was nothing but a complex crew of biological space cadets. Once their ship was off the ground, they had proceeded to cajole, color, rank, play off against, condemn, investigate, experiment, consort and fall in love with one another like any other random batch of humans being human.

Sometimes, even now, years later, I like to get together with Wes Jacobs, a staunch survivor of that era, and talk about the time Dr. Allen—who used to get juiced at lab parties—did a striptease, or the time when ethanol theft grew to such proportions that she had to send down a order that its use be strictly regulated. I've never forgotten that it was chemist and former winemaker Jack Murchio who introduced me to the work of novelist George P. Elliot and the writings of Alfred Döblin, the German Expressionist novelist who wrote *Alexanderplatz Berlin*. It was also around that time that I heard Ken Fishler play piano—the other of those lab aides named Ken—long before he joined with his singing wife to form the duo known as Bobbi & I, and also before he went on the road with singer Anita O'Day.

Betcha you never played "Green Onions," Kenny. But I did. I stole and stuck it—vamp chords, that is—directly into a song arrangement. That was around the time in my life when things started falling into place, when being around systematic processes of analysis infiltrated some mindless part of me to the point where I'd get flashes now and then, usually when showering to go to work, that we were all formed of earth and spirit and had as our goal the realization that, like a rainbow of flames in a Bunsen burner, we were emanating from the same ignited pilot.

RUBY MY DEAR
Thelonious Monk, 1959

You are back again, re-entering the central train of trails: the quintessential U.S.A. of drowsy fields and sleepy fastfood chains; the U.S.A. of nipped buds and layaways negotiated in harsh, flatland cracker accents. Surrounded by them, hemmed in, you sometimes feel a little like one of those brainy slicksters over at the Federal Penitentiary in Milan, Michigan, for, like them, you're locked up and keyed down.

"Ruby My Dear" comes drifting down Lake Huron in the saline marshlands of an eternal summer. The midwestern night is steamy hot with mosquitoes, the air knotted and thick with gnats like Monk's gracefully gnarled chordal clusters; notes and spiraling nodes, encoded, glistening like Milky Way-encrusted swirls and specks of darkness.

You know what you're hearing is human yearning, and rushes of the Divine calling you home to all the Africanized galaxies in this shimmering island universe.

COLD SWEAT

James Brown, 1967

"Excuse me while I do the boogaloo!"

Outrageous!

I couldn't believe it!

I sat riveted behind the wheel, realizing at last why those pantyhose packagers had the insight and audacity to name their product Sheer Energy.

Sheer energy was what James Brown was pushing; pushing and pulling and radiating in ultra-violet concentric circles of thermo-radiant funk. It was sheer energy with a whole lot of soul and blues slipped in—or, rather, *thrown* in the way you might sell somebody a 45 rpm disk or a .45 pistol—in this case, it doesn't matter—and throw in a shiny new Peterbilt truck for good measure, for the hell of it.

I was so carried away by the blues-grounded yet floating, gritty glide of it that I pulled the car I was driving off to some side street curb, cut the engine, cranked up the radio volume and just sat there, steaming in the warmth of that afternoon to let myself be swayed and lilted and swooshed away by the James Brown sound.

James Brown and the Famous Flames. He had that right too; the band was on fire. I sat in the car, my limbs going limp, sweat popping out of my forehead. I rolled the windows down in time to catch a lazy, passing breeze. That's when it hit me.

Right then and there the whole arrangement was etched into my burning brain; I soaked it all up—blowzy blue lines, vine-like rhythm, the works. It happened so fast and took so completely that when I found myself out on a dance floor at a party a few nights later, all I had to do when "Cold Sweat" came on was combine what I'd absorbed with the feeling of the moment, and the movements and motions took care of themselves. The trance was complete. Me and my partner, we must've been glowing out there with the lights down low.

What it was was hypnosis; hypnosis by osmosis. The hips gyrate; the nose opens. There was nothing subtle about it. I can even remember sitting there in the car, thinking: "They oughtn't be broadcasting this thing to drivers of cars. In fact, they need to slap one of those warning blurbs on the record itself that says, 'Under no circumstances is this music to be listened to while driving or operating dangerous machinery!'" And even while we were dancing, working ourselves up into a fever, I kept flashing on those festive occasions in the Caribbean where, when funk grew too thick or the body heat too scalding, all you had to do was dash outside, race down to the seashore, peel off your duds and rush into the water to cool down.

"Cold Sweat," the first time I heard it, had me swaying so far out there in musical space I was ready to either melt into the upholstery or get out and dance all over the top of the car. And by the time James Brown and the brothers broke into their cries of "Give the drummer some!" my sticky, hot hands were already playing the dashboard as though it were a three-piece conga set.

"Funky as you wanna be!"

"Keep it right there!"

"Excuse me while I do the boogaloo!"

THE SIDEWINDER

Lee Morgan, 1965

After a hard day, a work day, a bad day, a sad day or a Saturday, he'd come home, pop open two ice cold cans of beer, empty them into a schooner-sized glass with a giant olive, sip a little of it, unbutton his shirt, kick off his shoes and put "The Sidewinder" on the turntable.

By the time the beer was half finished, the record would be almost over and he'd be feeling like himself again—private and powerful.

Sometimes he wondered about it. Was it the music or the beer that refreshed him? Or was it just being on his own turf again; that landscape inside of him surrounded by seas as vast as life itself, all of it longing to be voyaged forever?

All he could really pin down was the pegleg rhythm of it; the way the beat mixed in with the horns and the web-like piano to produce something he was so in need of hearing that he'd actually cancelled dates and excused himself from social engagements to lie on the rug in the middle of his miniscule apartment and listen to Lee Morgan on all those Blue Note albums.

To him it was amazing, the flashes of say-so, the swagger, Morgan's sun-washed nerve, his urban innocence on ballads, the beat melting, pliant to the spirit he breathed into it. And all he really knew about the man was that Lee Morgan, like Clifford Brown, was another of those musical prodigies from the City of Brotherly Love. Along the grapevine word had traveled of his marriage to a Tokyo woman, someone he'd fallen in love with while touring Japan with Buhania, with Art Blakey's indefatigable Jazz Messengers. Morgan and his love came back to America and got married. He was happier than he'd ever been in his slender life, but his wife grew unhappy; she didn't speak much English and felt alienated. She missed her Land of the Rising Sun and soon flew out of his life to go back there.

Morgan was devastated and for well over a year wandered around New York feeling forlorn and uprooted. Then he married a Caribbean woman, someone older than himself. It didn't work out; tempers soared; there was misunderstanding, sorrow, a row; some kind of Frankie and Johnnie commotion. Then one night while he was on the stand at some club in New York, Morgan's new wife rushed in in mid-performance, stood off to the side in the crowd, pulled a revolver, took dead aim and squeezed the trigger.

Blam!

She didn't miss.

Another jazz great was nipped in the bud; wiped out cold in the heated bloom of life.

He missed Lee Morgan, but went on listening to "The Sidewinder" for years. The loping melody with its sloweddown Charleston accents kept going on in his world, relaxing him regularly by degrees. As far as he was concerned, Morgan could have titled it "The Unwinder." He loved it when jazz people got themselves a hit, and this one had to be a hit because it was moving in the stores and he heard it on the radio all the time.

After years of hosting the song in his bloodstream, he became curious about it and wanted to know what it meant. Late one afternoon, following a grueling day of work, he pulled out his *American Heritage Dictionary of the English*

Language and turned to the word *sidewinder* and found that it was "(1) A small rattlesnake, *croatalus cerastes,* of the Southwestern United States and Mexico, that moves by a distinctive lateral looping motion of its body; (2) A powerful blow delivered from the side; (3) *Military.* A short-range supersonic air-to-air missile."

He was shaken. All this time he had never given the term much thought, although, somewhere along the upper reaches of his over-worded poet's mind, he'd given it the meaning of a sidways punch or, sillier yet, he'd vaguely and privately associated it with the kind of electric emotionality that made one side of a record wind around and around. He really hadn't been ready to deal with the violent overtones of its triple meaning as they connected to Morgan's troubled lovelife and his sudden dismissal from this earth.

He stopped listening to "The Sidewinder" altogether and, for a long time, focused increasingly on the slow, flowing ballad side of his music-listening life.

Then the evening came when, easing his radio dial past an easy listening FM station—like a seasoned safecracker—he was slipped into the middle of a schmaltzy, mellow string orchestra performing "The Sidewinder." It surprised him to hear the snappy, syncopated strains of Lee Morgan's melody being played straight and literally in quasi-Muzak fashion. He couldn't believe that the piped-in elevator music community had picked up on the restful, energizing essences of Morgan's bluesy little popper.

He lay back, astonished, hands clasped behind his head, and wondered who was cashing the royalty checks.

18

MAIDEN VOYAGE

Herbie Hancock, 1969

Shhh, listen!

Can you hear it?

Listen. Listen. Shhh, it's like a soft, whispery, splashing sound. Symbolic. Cymbalic. It's a cymbal tap, the sound of wood barely touching a cymbal. The drummer's poised and ready to slip up on us. And the moment Herbie Hancock drops his fingers to the keyboard, real *pianissimo*, to sound that lovely, dark chord and four bass notes in tricky, off-accent time, we'll be off; we'll be on our way.

It's still astonishing, isn't it? What is time? I'm laying this down; you're picking it up. Everything happens at the same time. Ask any quantum physicist about the kind of dancing that goes on inside atoms, if you get my drift.

This time we'll be drifting over and across the Atlantic, sailing away from the Brooklyn Pier like an easy-going, recreational blimp in an amazing if not exactly good year. It just happens to be the very year they shot Medgar Evers in the back, the year they bombed that church in Birmingham and killed those little girls, the year the Russians put a woman in space, the year they marched 200,000 strong on Washington, D.C. and Martin Luther King and other black leaders met with the President, the year Defense Secretary

Diem started taking over the headlines, the year they were singing: "Aint gonna let nobody turn me round/turn me round/turn me round/Aint gonna let nobody turn me round/in Selma, Alabama!" while the governor was shouting: "Segregation forever!" It was the year they shot Kennedy down like a dog in Dallas. And when they started beating those little white kids, especially the girls, beating them with those billy-clubs the way they've always done colored people, you knew the American Century was coming home to roost.

Shhh, Herbie's just mashed down on the go-forward pedal; George Coleman is sounding the ship whistle. The waves are churning all around us and if you look closely you'll see me, a little brown speck of a speck in eternity, standing on the deck of a freighter pushing off from the Brooklyn Pier. It's the 28th of August, sunny and hot. Standing on the deck, waving at the workers on a ship from India docked next to ours, I'm growing a little bit sad and joyous at the same time as I picture myself atop the timeless ocean, pondering the vastness of my animal-wrapped soul and vision which I know I must cleanse of false learning before I can go the infinite way of Atlantics and Pacifics, Indian Oceans and Bering Seas. I stand there, watching the Statue of Liberty grow greener and tinier in the fog beginning to roll in now. "Roll with the boat," I'm remembering hearing somebody say. "Roll with the boat, don't fight it, and that way you won't get seasick."

We're rolling along right now with the beat, which isn't easy to pin down or measure, and all the ghosts outside our porthole ears seem to be carrying on in Portuguese. Timelessness, meanwhile, is enfolding and washing me clean on this maiden voyage.

Who am I?

What am I doing?

Where are we going?

All I am is daring. Absolutely. All I'm doing is drifting,

but don't take that to mean I lack a sense of direction. And, now that you ask, we're headed for Lisbon in the off-season of a year surcharged with political meaning, spiritual greening and love everlastingly leaning in the only direction there is.

There's something we need to get straight before we get to trumpeter Freddie Hubbard, before we even reach the high seas. Herbie hasn't even recorded "Maiden Voyage" yet. For all we know, he's still inking and dotting the tableted version of "Watermelon Man," his jubilant blues-to-riches hit. But he's around like I'm around and I can sense the musical counterpart of what I'm going through on this Portuguese freighter, dancing in the air all around us like ocean air and spume, those half-thoughts, dreams, hunches and hints and radiant inspirations. It's the same shock of inspiration that put me suddenly out there with those picketers and hellraisers during an earlier version of the March on Washington, fully four years before the big one that made newspaper and TV history. We came close to getting stomped, remember? The time that mounted police-man was about to spur his horse into rearing up and crushing us underfoot on the Washington Memorial Monu-ment Mall before that sidekick of his yelled: "Hey, hoss, calm down and let them kids live!" All we were doing was crowding around to wait for Harry Belafonte to come out and sing to us.

Remember too that, then as now, I was mostly thought, ideas, notions and drift. I even thought I had to grab hold of anything that went floating through my mind, either to act upon or pursue. I'm only slightly wiser than that now, but I can see quite clearly how I'd had it in my head for the longest to somehow beat my way to Europe. And magically there I was, finally doing it, equipped with nothing more than a steel-string guitar (a Gibson), a blue Navy surplus dufflebag crammed with clothing and books, and in my pockets there was something like $160 in Cook's Travelers Checques to last for who knew how long? What in the world?—

But craziness craves company. The other passengers on that off-season freighter helped keep me sane. Listen to how Freddie Hubbard gets caught up in those surf-riding arpeggios of his on the "Maiden Voyage" he took with Herbie Hancock. The ocean'll change you; you'll go out a nut— roasted, salted and ready to be crunched in the hard-bop molars of restlessness—and, after days and nights of rocking in rhythm and smooth sailing, you'll reach another shore, land on the other side, softly throbbing, restored to your shell, ready to curl up, surrender and stalk back to the very vine that nurtured and spawned you.

Along the way, like a basket-tray of music being passed around and played, you'll find yourself changing when you realize you've gotten yourself into one of the most illuminating of situations. Without thinking, you've booked yourself on a scaled down model of the planet itself. Suddenly the whole world's been reduced to everybody who happens to be on board. Surely that must have been what Texas-tetched story-teller Katherine Anne Porter had in mind when she spent close to 20 years writing that book she knowingly called *Ship of Fools*.

There was a chain-smoking old Portuguese-American married to someone who worked for the Portuguese Information Center in New York who used to sit on deck beside me and speak of nothing but how cheap leather and booze was in Spain. He even showed me his own painted belt. He called himself Charlie and he loved the States.

"We Americans," he once told me, "we are strong people, yes? The strongest next to West Germany—I dunno about the East. I am an American. My wife, no—she is Portuguese. 'Why be American?' she always say. I live in Bronx. You know where that is—uptown. In Portugal and in Spain you will see the *toros*, the best there is. In Spain they let you kill the bull. But not in Portugal. It's against the law. Me myself,

I rather see the bull killed than the man because you can eat the bull. He make good meat, no? But not the man. You cannot eat the man, ha ha hahahahahaha!"

There was an aged woman, a columnist for the *Ladies Home Journal,* who plied me with Dramamine. "I'm one of the best-paid magazine writers in the business," she told me. At the time she was getting $500 a throw for her submissions. "They say it's read by 7 million women all over the world." It seems she specialized in pieces on home and family life, short stories, anything she could come up with. "But now that my husband's dead," she went on, "and my family's grown up, I'm organizing my columns into a book, and I have to write another book on the life of my daughter who also died. It's for her children. I plan to spend the year in Lisbon." Then from out of nowhere she looked at me point-blank and said: "If you're a writer, where's your pad and pencil?"

"In my cabin," I shot back defensively.

"Then you may use my typewriter if you don't have one." And from then on during the course of that thoughtful exchange—between twitching attacks of obvious nausea— she carefully related the story of her publishing life, beginning with her college co-ed days when her father, a journalist, was something of a regional shaker and mover in midwestern Republican politics.

There was a bouncy, plump young woman who favored black—apparel, that is. She also liked to spruce her light-brown hair up with a pernicious bleached shock of blonde. She had a round, pink face and curious nostrils. When I told her Paris was my destination, she said she'd give me the name of a girlfriend who worked and lived there, who had a house.

"I met her," she explained, "when she worked for the Atomic Attaché in Washington. Did I see you bring an instrument aboard?—a guitar? Are you a folksinger? You must entertain us some night. My roommate used to date some famous folksingers. She was very interested in folk music. I happen to be going to Paris myself. Have you met the English lady aboard? She's from the British Consulate in Portugal. She's done so many things and travelled all over the world. She's gone on 39 safaris with her husband in Africa. You must meet her."

It just so happened I *had* met the English woman. She spoke lovely, nasal Portuguese and reminded me of Miss Sample, a severe homeroom and Spanish teacher from Hutchins Intermediate School days in Detroit who, with her delicate features and robins-egg knit dress, went into for blue-rinsing her white hair. From the way the English lady lifted her skirts whenever she was around the handsome first-mate, I could tell that whatever she'd gone through with that husband of hers hadn't chilled the natural woman in her.

One afternoon following lunch when a trio of us had climbed up to the first-mate's quarters, he asked me if I knew how to play "Tequila" on guitar, that tired hit single by The Champs. I donned my fingerpicks and struck up the tune, which really wasn't much more than a Latin-accented rhythmic vamp broken up every few bars by the spirited interjection of the word *tequila!* The first-mate, who had dragged the English lady up to dance in what tiny, cramped space there was, pronounced it *teh-kee-ya!* And when, in classic, uncool macho fashion, he removed his shirt to bare his sweaty, hairy chest, the lady from England, flushed with afternoon wine, giggled and cried: "I feel like taking something off too!"

Thus did we all take off, oddballs each of us, on a journey that now exists in mind alone. In no time—and largely because word got around the ship at once that I was something of an entertainer—I got to know everybody on board; everybody, that is, except the Ship's Captain and a pair of mousey nuns, two young missionary women who also happened to be sisters, siblings.

The Captain, who looked as if he'd just stepped right off the Lipton's Tea package, never invited me to have dinner with him as he did all the other passengers. It hurt me at first, but gradually I concluded that he had funny feelings about people of color. As for the nuns, those pale-faced Americans who spent most of the trip in their cabin stricken with seasickness, they disapproved of drinking, smoking, music, dancing, bingo and liveliness in general. In short, they were down on all those activities that made the crossing socially workable. I had a hard time picturing how they were going to instill religion in the "savages" in the wilds of Angola to which they'd been dispatched by their dreary mission. Secretly I'd catch myself pulling for rough sailing that would keep them locked away in their quarters, protected, so to speak, from the rest of us.

I had some favorites, though, among the passengers and crew. There was a hearty gent named Silvanho who always tuned up at my table on the first call to breakfast, lunch or dinner. At every meal, the Portuguese, I found, ate like horses. I was known, in those days of skin and boniness, to put away some grub, but all that codfish *bacalao* and sautéed potatoes and vegetables and fruit and wine, lavishly drenched in olive oil, finally got to me. But Silvanho, all of 60 years of age, tall and solidly constructed, ate and ate and ate. He was the one who taught me how to peel fruit with a knife so that the skin got removed in one elegant, civilized spiral of a coil. He was a landscaper based in Massachusetts and this was his fourth crossing. Even the bald part of his head glistened tan and golden—I attributed it to liberal intakes of olive oil and garlic—in the midst of fluffy, gray locks. He told me he was married to the ex-wife of some ambassador. She had lost everything in the Second World War, so they were poor. Silvanho had children by a woman in Massachusetts, but none by his wife. He was anxious to get to Madeira, the capital of Funchal in the Azores Islands where we'd be stopping before continuing on to Lisbon.

"You married?" he asked me.

"No."

"Ah, that's wonderful. You do anything you want, go wherever you like. That's the way!"

"How long you planning to stay on Madiera?"

"Don't know. Maybe for good. I rather be buried there than in the United States."

I knew right away that he hoisted bright snifters of brandy all day long, but it took me a couple of days to find out he played harmonica.

"Hey," he said one night. "You and me. You play guitar, I play harmonica, and I teach you *fados*. Do you know what is *fado*?"

I told him I knew it was the Portuguese version of the Argentine tango, something like my people's folk music called blues.

"Exactly," he said, "and I teach you the *fado*, two or three *fados* and in two or three nights we play them together in the *sala de fumar* before bingo. There is a lady, the one who is English, I wish to conquer with love songs."

We practiced, rehearsed and performed like champions, but he never got far with the English woman who, I'd learned by then, had married a man close to 60 when she was 20. He was wealthy, which accounted for all those safaris they'd been on in Africa. According to her, the days were never long enough for them to say all they had to say to one another. He died at the age of 89, and she was still attending his grave once a week to "tell him everything." Born in Portugal, she had visited England several times—always on holiday—and the U.S. only once, and recently at that. She loved to drink and dance and talk trash to the men.

Finding out the nit and grit of what lay beneath everyone's skin prompted me to begin taking deep looks at the relationship of soul to fleshly entrapment and what better situation than an ocean voyage to do it? "Desire binds man to earth," Gary Snyder had written in his book of poems,

Riprap, packed in my dufflebag, and I was beginning to see how that Buddhistic truism worked.

The woman who wrote for the *Ladies Home Journal*, for instance, was given to showing me clippings of articles she'd penned, and she was singularly proud of an illustration Norman Rockwell had done to illustrate a story of hers. Most of her writing had been done long before my time. When I thought about her during sleepless, porthole-hungry hours, I found her sad, noting that writing was all she had to show for an otherwise colorless life. Then and there I determined I was never going to separate my writing life from myself, and that risks, whatever danger taking them entailed, were something I'd never rule out.

Among the crew, I grew fond of Marx, the man my own age who tended the cabins, who knew a great deal about passengers' personal habits and vices since he was the one who took orders for liquor and tobacco and also passed the stuff out. Marx—don't ask me how he came by his name—told me that he loved his job because it kept him out of Salazar's Portugal for long periods. He loved his country, but was profoundly saddened by the tyrannical regime that had been governing and milking it for all too long. He was also busy studying English on his own and read a lot. I've never forgotten the morning following breakfast when I ran into him coming out of my cabin which he'd just finished tidying.

"Senhor," he said with his curly-headed, boyish face of a smile, "you drink too much brandy, much too much for a man so young in years."

"Do you really think so?" I said, startled.

"Yes, and I do not understand why. The old men, yes, I understand the sadness of why they drink, but you, no. Are you so unhappy?"

"No, no I don't really think I am."

"You play the guitarra and sing so happy, and you write, yes?"

27

"I write a lot, yes."

"What do you write?"

"Oh, poetry and stories and I keep a journal."

Marx's handsome face seemed to brighten with heightened comprehension when I told him this. "I must arrange that you meet the ship nurse. He too writes in a how-you-say journal. Very funny man, very funny. This, ah, journal of his, it is big, very big—25 big notebooks."

"Oh," I said, delighted, "I must see it!"

Marx shrugged and shook his head indifferently. "I do not understand this journal business. It is crazy. When he is writing in his notebooks and he look up and see a satellite go by up in the sky, then he write on his page: 'While I write I look up and see a satellite in the sky.' Writers, they are funny. Do you read this prisoner, this man who write a book in California at prison, but who commit the murders?"

"What's the name of the book?"

All of this sea-going talk, mind you, was being carried on in Portuguese and Spanish with little bursts of English.

Marx screwed up his face in all seriousness and, in curious English, said: "It is called *The Kayeed Waz a Kailler.*"

I pondered this while Marx stared at me intently, waiting for his long-shot, homemade pronunciation to somehow hit home.

"Aha!" I shot back at last. "You mean, *The Kid Was a Killer.* Caryl Chessman, yes?"

"Sim, sim," he cried, "that is it, that is it! Now, how you say it in real English?"

We laughed and then talked about Chessman in our babbling stew of a lingo. It struck me for the first time that people in different parts of the world could be in tune and care about one another on a highly accurate, static-free frequency without necessarily knowing how to put it in words.

But language helped and, as I hung over the railing morning after morning, inhaling the sea and sky and, in my

But language helped and, as I hung over the railing morning after morning, inhaling the sea and sky and, in my lightened head, beholding the past as if it were a sharply experienced dream, I couldn't help but realize how all the interest I'd taking in getting to know bits and pieces of other languages seemed to foretell that I'd be taking this trip. Ah, there's nothing like all that wind and water to help you recall the root meaning of everything you've ever thought or done. I was up on deck, regaling in this one day when a portly old crewman with a beret pulled snugly across his head approached me with a smile as big as the universe and proceeded to flap his arms at his sides and squeal and grunt in imitation of a walrus. He even yelled out the Portuguese word for walrus—*morsa*—and pointed at himself to indicate that this was, in fact, him. One glance at his drooping, gray, thick mustache and hooded eyes was enough to confirm and corroborate the likeness.

It wasn't long after this that Walrus, who proudly showed me his many volumes of diaries—all penned in admirably neat Portuguese with pictures and clippings from magazines pasted in meaningfully—decided it was high time I met the ship's cook. It was a Saturday afternoon. The Atlantic was very South Pacific-like; it was calm. That's all he said, that I should meet the cook.

Actually, the cook and I had been taking peeps at one another from the moment I'd climbed aboard, but, coming as I was from the States, I never suspected he was the one in charge of the kitchen. Cultural brainwashing runs deep. He was a thin-boned black man of slight build in soiled white apron and chef's cap who put me in mind of Mance Lipscomb. Suddenly it became impossible to ignore that we were brothers of the skin greeting one another.

"You Americano?" he said.

"Si," I said, still Spanish-oriented. Right away he broke into Portuguese and I rushed to explain right off I could yak in Spanish far better than I could in Portuguese, slipping in a friendly *"Usted entiende el Español?"*

"Ah, *Sim*! You go Lisboa?"

"Sim," I said, *"entonces a Madrî."* (Yeah, then on to Madrid.)

He smiled and shook his head yes.

Then, because I'd run out of things to say, I told him: *"Las comidas por aquí son muy buenas."* (The chow around here's great.)

The little cook laughed, obviously understanding everything I wasn't able to say so didn't try. He waved heartily, one traveler of African descent to the other.

There we stood, perceptible in memory alone, looking into one another as if we were mirrors; looking into one another with a careful gentleness that seemed to telepathically affirm our secret identities as ghostly figments, fragments, mere passing specks in a diaspora whose naturalizing influence and effect on the rest of mankind has been growing with the millenia, widening and deepening with every cymbal swish and each impassioned breath thrust into a vibratory mouthpiece or the flicker or flick of finger laid to rest against valve or key. Music, like thought or remembrance, was sloshing or rocking or frothing around and around us like the ocean itself, that watery tomb that reputedly spawned our species.

And on we sailed that way for days and days. Divisions between day and night gradually mattered less and less; waking consciousness began to merge with dream consciousness. Before long I was identifying with the ocean as neighborhood and eternal verity. All mankind, as far as I was concerned, resided right there on that boat which I began to vaguely view as Noah's Ark. We might not've been paired up two by two, yet the realness of the notion that everything has its opposite in this gnashing, splashing, miraculous environment, the ocean, drove me home. And where exactly was home? It certainly wasn't there in the

Azores, nor was it in listless Lisbon. It was all crammed and situated right there in my own heart of hearts.

Listening to Hancock's "Maiden Voyage" washes it all ashore, that electrifying storehouse of memory, spoken and unspoken, whose kaleidoscopic message boiled down to this: We are only dribs and drabs and particles and waves in an infinite sea of possibilities. It's possible, for example, to step on a slow boat to China or any other distant destination and step off of it the epitome of newness; a whole other being.

I loved that.

I love the way Herbie Hancock took the sweet time to sit down and put it all in music which is nothing if it isn't a sisterly companion to its solemn brother mathematics.

By the time we reached Lisbon, where I was duly trailed and haunted by the Secret Police in Hollywood trenchcoats, I'd shaken myself loose from a lifetime of longing. Belonging to myself and to something vaster than I could ever possibly conceive, I felt like dancing the fado all over the Iberian Peninsula and, although my shipmates had grown strangely aloof and impersonal when we disembarked to traipse toward customs, I knew I'd always remember my own first crossing. "Maiden Voyage" won't let me forget it.

The seeing sea can seed and seize you ceaselessly. And even when its melody subsides, the harmony it lines out within our inner ear is enough to make you want to sing along out loud and jump for joy.

And you don't even have to climb aboard a boat to feel it.

Shhh, listen!

Can you hear it?

Cup a simple seashell to your ear.

Now.

Can you hear it, can you hear it?

BREEZIN'

George Benson, 1976

The Text

Anyone who caught the recent **PBS TV** special, *The World of John Hammond,* couldn't help but be moved by George Benson's splendid cameo performance with the reconstructed Benny Goodman Sextet.

At one point, during a gently heated rendition of "7 Come 11," the perennially elegant "King of Swing" himself, clarinet in hand, broke out into a broad, unabashed grin in the middle of Benson's joyously plucked solo. It was, for all too fleeting a moment, as if the living spirit of another celebrated Goodman sideman, the Oklahoma trailblazer Charlie Christian, who abandoned this world at the poetic age of 23, had taken possession of this exciting guitarist.

George Benson has been around for some time. Jazz devotees from his native Pittsburgh were singing his praises years ago, back when he was working what was then known as the Chitlin & Gravy Circuit in that hard-working, music-loving city.

He was 19 years old when he joined veteran grit organist Jack McDuff's group in the 1960s. Before that, having played guitar since the age of 8, he'd sung in a rhythm and blues combo led by his cousin. This is a strong tip, for it indicates that Benson's playing has long been rooted in both the blues and black popular song, musical idioms which—like blues, jazz and pop in general—have tended to vitally affect one another down through the years.

Besides leading his own bands, Benson has worked and recorded with an impressive roster of outstanding artists who are as varied in esthetic sensibility as saxophonists Hank Crawford and Stanley Turrentine, singer Esther Phillips, and trumpeters Freddie Hubbard and Miles Davis. His playing, though, has always been distinguished by a good feeling and high energy that are his alone.

There appear to be fewer and fewer jazz musicians to whom one can look for relaxed, inspired playing these days. George Benson still delivers.

The Notes

You never know what's going to hit. There are ships coming in and ships going out, and in the record business everybody's pretty much at sea most of the time, particularly the lowly annotator of album jackets. Often he or she is called upon to work what virtually amounts to magic without really knowing what the musicians, producers or the record companies have up their sleeves.

Such was the case with George Benson's illustrious *Breezin'* album. One day I got a phonecall from Charlie Haas down in L.A. who was working at the time for Warner Bros. Records. "Al," he said, "I know you're busy, but do you think you could find time to write some liner notes for a George Benson LP we're putting together?"

At the time I was, indeed, under tremendous pressure to earn my wings in freelance heaven. As usual, I was tied up with several projects at once: a screenplay, editing a new issue of *Yardbird Reader,* the multicultural literary journal I'd founded with poet-novelist Ishmael Reed, a magazine article or two, book reviews for the *New York Times,* a new novel-in-progress, some poems as always, and preparation for the last class I'd be teaching at Stanford University. To tell the truth, I was about as crazed as they come, and yet I got back to Charlie right away and told him I'd be thrilled to somehow try and squeeze the Benson LP into my schedule.

Days later a pair of reel-to-reel tapes arrived in the mail. They were the basic tracks of Benson handling lead guitar and vocals, the amazing Phil Upchurch on rhythm guitar, Ronnie Foster on electric piano and mini-moog, Jorge Dalto on clarinet and acoustic piano, Stanley Banks on bass, Harvey Mason and Ralph MacDonald holding down drums and percussion respectively. That was all. Claus Ogerman's orchestral sweetenings had yet to be recorded and mixed by engineer Al Schmitt. Quite literally, what I had to work from in making my notes had no strings attached.

I listened and listened and listened and listened and finally sat down one sunny afternoon and pecked out what eventually came to be the text of that award-winning, bronze album. Benson's soulful interpretation of Leon Russell's "This Masquerade" became a hit all unto itself and the record sold so well—millions of copies—that I began to fantasize about how rich I myself might've become had I told Charlie Haas from the very beginning that, rather than accept a flat fee for my simple notes, I'd settle for a mere half cent per unit sold. Warner Bros. Records would never have gone for it, but I certainly would've made a sweet piece of change on the deal.

As it turned out, *Breezin'* launched George Benson's career as a pop star and set him up as one of the most commercially successful black crossover performers since Louis Armstrong. It couldn't have happened to a nicer guy. A handsome, superbly gifted artist who also happens to be a devout Seventh Day Adventist, Benson quietly shattered the myth that you had to dissipate, starve or go mad to get over as a jazz musician. This isn't to say he hasn't paid his dues and isn't still paying.

I'm still paying my respects to *Breezin'* since, in an

unexpected and even laughable sort of way, the album put a bit of my writing right up under the noses of millions of browsers—and quite possibly a few readers as well—all over the world. Following years of sweating out novels, articles, poetry and invisible scripts, all it took was an afternoon of loving yet solemnly composed prose commentary to establish me back home, on old familial grounds, as having amounted to something after all. It's a moment I'll always cherish.

The time: 1976.

The place: My younger sister Aveda's home in Ann Arbor, Michigan; she's introducing me to a roomful of her friends.

The line: "This is my brother Albert who lives in California. He wrote the stuff on the back of that George Benson *Breezin'* album."

The response: "Oh, you the one wrote that? Man, that's beautiful, beautiful! Lemme shake your hand. It isn't everyday you get to shake hands with a real writer!"

The moral: There's no business like show business.

MERCEDES-BENZ

Janis Joplin, 1969

Janis, your song and my Sadies arrived the same year!

For $600 you couldn't beat it: a sparkling 220 Mercedes-Benz sedan in the darkest of midnight blue shades that the light would hit and make gleam just like one of those old British detective cars I used to admire in old J. Arthur Rank films of 1950s vintage; the kind of no-nonsense motor car Rita Tushingham seemed perfectly comfortable hopping in and out of between serio-comic episodes of a romantic story with a bittersweet twist.

I knew when I plunked my money down that I could've been buying a lemon. But when Adam and Lois Miller told me about that car one Saturday night at a sweltering dance party, I coolly made up my mind that very moment that they were right when they'd said: "This car's for you; it's you through and through. It's just the machine for a writer with a flare for simple elegance!"—or words to that special effect.

A few days later I boogie'd right up to the Oakland Hills and offered to buy the automobile from the owner who had it parked in front of his house with one of those regulation red and white *FOR SALE* signs displayed in one of the rear passenger windows. He was an uptight, prejudiced foothills resident who, I could tell right off, wasn't exactly ecstatic about the idea of selling his treasured, almost-classic vehicle to a mere Negro. Refusing to take my personal check, he insisted that I either bring cash or a certified bank draft to his place of business for the precise amount the following day. It just so happened he was an auto mechanic. Adam Miller, who had gone with me to check the car over, knew the score. I knew the score. Even though we were both black and professionally literate, we were still Americans. I wanted to call the whole thing off. Adam, who'd owned a Mercedes for years, said: "Just go and get the money and bring it to the bastard, then you'll have yourself a good car, OK?" I took his advice.

And what a car it was! It still had its original paint job from 1956, shiny chrome trimmings, white-wall tires (or ought I say *tyres?*), wood panel work along the dashboard and doors, attractively worn and partially cracked leather seats in a soft, dove gray upholstery; fog lights, scientific-looking meters and gauges, bucket seats, and thick floor carpeting. In short, it had all the right stuff to make you feel every bit as virtuous and glamorous as people treated you once you got behind that wheel, mashed down on the accelerator and started tooling around town. I went right out too and invested in fancy car waxes to while away many a Saturday and Sunday afternoons working like a coolie to make my foreign car shine.

Snappy. That was the word. It was easily the snappiest-looking car I've ever owned. Remember, you're getting this from someone who didn't start driving until he was well into his twenties; someone who had previously owned a $50 Ford and a $200 American Motors Rambler Wagon. In that respect, I was anything but American; if anything, I was a thorough discredit to a nation of auto users and abusers.

Suddenly, though, I was something to be reckoned with. By dint of installing myself behind the wheel of what most people considered to be a luxury car, I was initiated at once into the grand scheme of things automotive according to which people do not ask "Is this your car?" but, rather, "Is this you?"

Is this you? That was the key. No, it wasn't me; it could never be me. It was only an almost antique auto I oughtn't have been fooling with in the first place, but the impression I gave off was that of a well-heeled, successful oddball who just happened to be driving one of Germany's finest industrial products in a country that measured human worth on the basis of an individual's material accumulations.

Was that Mercedes me? For awhile I thought it was; I wanted so for it to be me. How keenly I recall parking it in front of a San Francisco bookstore I've frequented for years and having one of the hip clerks rush out and shout: "Why, Al Young, you slick sonofabitch! So you finally sold out!" Or the afternoon I happened to be chatting on the street with another Mercedes owner who also happened to be my color. There we stood at curbside, leaning against our cars, when a derelict white man stumbled by across the street. He stood for a minute, staring at us, then cupped his hands to his mouth and screamed at the top of his ugly voice: "Hey! Hey! You niggers think you're takin over the world, don't you? You think you got everything sewed up! Well, you know what? Fuck you, you black assholes! Fuck every one of you black nigger bastards!"

Then there were the black people themselves who put me through changes. There was the hefty highway patrolman who pulled me over one summer evening, stomped around the sedan, checking every part of that car out, finally leaning over the hood and fingering the windshield wipers.

"I'm giving you a citation," he said at last.

"A citation for what?"

"Faulty windshield wipers!"

"May I ask what's wrong with the windshield wipers?"

"Sure, you can ask."

"Then, tell me, how are they faulty?"

"They're just faulty, that's all! You got that? Your

windshield wipers are faulty! Now, you wanna get belligerent? I been pretty nice to you up till now."

And there were the dents and nicks and the stealing of the Mercedes chrome insignia that customarily graces the front of the hood. Sometimes you felt as if people went out of their way to do bodily harm to your car simply because it was supposed to be a luxury car. It wasn't unusual, for instance, to climb back inside of it at some parking garage to find that the car had been broken into and burglarized.

Mercedes-Benz repairmen—those immaculately garbed gentlemen in greaseless smocks—would take one look at me and sense intuitively that I had no business trying to maintain such a car. In fact, when the oil pump finally blew on the freeway one day and I had to have the car towed by Triple A to the nearest German auto garage, I was informed, forthright and bluntly, that the cost for repairing the frozen pistons was probably going to run higher than the value of the car. "And if you cannot afford to pay our fee," said the head mechanic, "then we want the thing towed from our premises within 48 hours. Do you understand?" I understood. Moreover, I was required to sign a prepared, written statement to that effect.

Oh, Janis, it was all too much! The next time you put in a request in your prayerful song for a Mercedes-Benz, be sure and ask the Lord to throw in some upkeep money to boot. And, while you're at it, you just might want to picture me leaving that alien garage on foot, walking two blocks to the closest bus stop, stepping aboard, plopping down in a window seat and sighing while I thought to myself: "Ahhh, good riddance! That's one more possession that won't be possessing me no more!"

I got myself a brand new Datsun 510 Wagon and drove back into the future.

CHEROKEES

Al Young, 1966
(CHEROKEE, Ray Noble 1936;
KO KO, Charlie Parker, 1944)

Brave Indian warrior
I'm gld I sawr ya
Now, that's the way I like to start singing *Cherokee* which
is a fine song I think and one day I shall learn all the words.

Ray Noble, an Englishman, wrote Cherokee long before I
dropped into the century. I can't help wondering what kind
of waves his mind or heart might have been radiating at the
time.

Historical Note: "In 1762 three Cherokee chiefs appeared
in London as picturesque ambassadors. Indian reprisals for
acts of lawless frontiersmen had marred English-Cherokee
relations; but a year after the Indians' visit to England,
whites and reds signed a treaty of friendship," it says in *The
American Heritage Book of Indians*.

Ah, the unlikeliness of world lore. It was Charlie Parker of
course who first pulled me into the song itself on his faithful
old Savoy recording of it when I was a dreamy adolescent
addicted to the various musicks. Nights I'd sit in my window
and behold that tune growing brighter and brighter in the
light of all that light Mr. Parker kept bringing to it. He
called it *Ko-Ko*, and all the famous jazz writers like to re-jot
what Mr. Parker told them was in his mind and heart around

the time he was getting his ideas about *Cherokee* together, starting around December 1939 (I'd been back on Earth six months): Bird's in the backroom of that Harlem Chili House "jamming" with Biddy Fleet the guitar player, so Bird, quite naturally, like each of God's creations, has a very special message he has been getting ready to drop in the public for quite some time. "I could hear it sometimes but I couldn't play it!"

Then he got on into *Cherokee*.

History.

It's all history. We're all history.

The trees and stones are history.

Moon is history.

It all keeps meeting at the moment, yet we are fond of believing ourselves to be the center of all creation.

To further simplify matters, Cherokee is also the name of one of God's creations I first heard about after school when all the kids would stand around the doors and highwire fence to smoke cigarettes and make fun of everything—which is becoming standard behavior for children when they're no more than 13 or 14 years in the world.

This girl I knew would say, "Well, what I like about Cherokee is he got a whole lot of soul, know what I mean? Cherokee look you dead in your eye when he talk and he pretty sincere too about what he gon do—if he go for you. Like, the time he told Mr. Crookshank right out loud in class, told him right to his face he was prejudiced and he was gon personally whip his butt first chance he got, so Mr. Crookshank get all uptight and jiggedy and take Cherokee up to the principal and tell him what Cherokee say, tell him this boy threatened me in class, so Mr. Brown ask Cherokee did he really say that, so Cherokee say, 'That's correct, you heard right, I mo go up side this gentleman's head if he dont start having some respect for all us students irregardless of race, color or creed.' "

"Yeah and what about that time he stole the police car over on Linwood while the cops was sittin up in Stafford's eatin dinner and there was Cherokee ridin up and down the block playin the siren and when the cops come out to see who it was they dont find out nothin cause by that time Cherokee done eased the short on round the corner and parked it and gone on bout his business"—

"Unnh-hunh, I knew about that but what about the time over at the Greystone Ballroom when Cool Breeze and Captain Midnight and them was drinkin all that bad wine talkin bout how they was go turn the place out in a few minutes soon as they drink some more wine and Cool Breeze talkin bout he was so bad and got two brothers run with The Shakers* and then after they finish drinkin wine they started messin with Cherokee's broad, man, Rennie, and you know Cherokee he pretty peaceful till people get to messin over him and he know Cool Breeze and them is drunk so he tell em they better be cool, so then they wouldn't stop so Cherokee snatch they little bottle of wine away from em and him and his boys turns out the Greystone in 15-20 minutes, and Cool Breeze and Captain Midnight and them was supposed to be so bad—"

His girlfriend Rennie (Renée) lived not too far from me: a lean, comely redheaded gal whose mama'd get drunk and beat her up all the time or lock her out of the house when she'd come in too late. Rennie luhhhved Cherokee and was wise to the fact that any of the ordinary girls would gratefully walk from Windsor, Ontario all the way to Detroit, Michigan to say "Hi" to him anyday. Rennie herself was no ordinary young lady. She always figured that if push came to shove she could always strut those freckles on out to Hollywood and sign up as a starlet. "My old lady dont dig me because she knows I'm cute, but that's all right—long as I got Cherokee."

Cherokee's thing seemed to be to show up for classes when there was absolutely nothing else doing. You'd see him and then he'd be gone. First time I saw him, someone else was pointing him out to me. "Well, there he go, man."

"There go who?"

"There go Cherokee."

"So that's Cherokee."

"That is *the* Cherokee, you mean to tell me you didnt know who Cherokee was?"

"Look, I feel like I was born knowin Cherokee but I only just now switched over to this school a little while ago."

"Well, *I'll* excuse you but if I was you I wouldnt go round tellin too many people I didnt know who Cherokee was."

"O I know who he was all right, I just wasnt sure which one he was."

"Cherokee been tryna get outta this Junior High School a whole lot longer'n it's taken you to get in."

"What's the matter with him?"

"He aint got good sense."

"How come?"

"How come you ask me somethin like that. Man, I dont know—he just aint got good sense. He a Indian, maybe Indians aint suppose to have good sense. Of course he part Spook too. I dont know, but I tell you one thing: dont nobody be messin with him."

So much for hearsay. I met up with him in an art class one semester and he was very quiet and dutiful, did his little drawings, always had a good word for everyone, took his work very seriously. Then he went and got into another one of those bizarre situations and was thrown out of school again. Fortunately, I ran up on him again at La Fiesta, a short-lived non-Mexican rib parlor on 12th Street. He bought me Pepsi Cola and he said, "Man, I like you. Guess you see me all the time gettin into trouble with my mouth and fightin and carryin on but I know what I wanna do. I wanna do the same thing everybody else wanna do, you know? Wanna just be cool, you know? Just draw and sing and stuff and get along with everybody and be cool. That aint askin too much is it? But the people wont leave me alone, look like all they wanna do's keep messin with me. But you just wait and see, just keep watchin, man, I mo make it. I shall be cool and do my thing dont care how long it take. I'm in a little trouble right now but that wont stop me."

A few months later Cherokee got busted—I forget for what—burglary or something—and was sent away to be reformed. I have never seen him again, but everytime I hear the song or get to whistling it, I often flicker back thru dreams to that April afternoon to the exact place where he removed his shades and looked me dead in the eye to say, "I'm in a little trouble right now but that wont stop me."

I was also reminded of him when a middle-aged Cherokee Indian on the no. 43 bus to Oakland last Christmas told the dark little girl plopped by me, says, "Ha ha, you a Nigger, you don't come from here, your people don't come from here, you not like me, you from Africa."

So she huffs herself up gently and says: "And just where do you think you come from?"

He was drunk.
We are all drunk
with self-hatred
one time or another,
how else can we go on
hating one another?

*A major gang in the history of Detroit, from the 1950s.

44

THE YEARS
WITH MILES

One night, a wintry Sunday in the country of Seattle, I went for a walk and ended up bewitched in a record shop in the University District. To promote a "comeback concert" that never took place, the store was running a discount sale on all of Miles Davis's stuff. I'd been listening to his Columbia album, *The Man With the Horn* on the radio, gone out to clear my head, seen the LP in the shop window and—haunted by thoughts of incipient middleage—ducked right inside to shake the cold.

Positioned at the D's in the alphabetized jazz section, I flipped through dozens of Miles Davis LPs, finding it tough to believe I knew most of them by heart. Even more surprising was my instant realization that the music compressed in those vinyl grooves had played a strange and indefinable role in shaping me and the years I'd grown up in; years that saw me wobble down from the hills of adolescence toward the slippery banks of maturity.

Photos of Miles and inspired graphics gracing the albums were suddenly telling me stories. I couldn't tell if they were stories I'd originally spun around myself when I'd first listened to a given piece of Miles's music or whether I was now a character in the stories I'd told. The experience was, I suppose, a little like poring over a forgotten stash of family snapshots and portraits. When you do that, you aren't necessarily seeing or registering pictures and images. Often you're looking beyond to another vision altogether; an inner vision of feeling, emotional states or mini-dramas whose meanings can never truly be clear to anyone but you.

Such is the tricky, highly private process of memory, and such was my delight in rediscovering how much that eccentric man's musical communication had meant to me.

It isn't even easy to say when my deep affection for Miles's playing and the many groups he's led actually began to develop. I like to believe it's always been there, fully blown, like spring rain or summer storms. Hindsight, though, tells me differently. Increasingly, recall is mostly what I go by, and, since recall is as vulnerable and mercurial as emotion, I keep finding myself spread-legged beside an ocean, remembering how long the sea itself has been around and how it must have begun at some point or other. And you know what that means, don't you? Even the history of a sound in your mind, in your heart, in all parts of your powerful invisibility, and your aural imagination above all, must have begun somewhere, at a single point.

TEMPUS FUGIT, 1953

With Don and Al Wardlow, musical brothers and bebop buddies of mine, I skip school to go see Frank Sinatra as drummer Frankie Machine in the film version of Nelson Algren's *The Man with the Golden Arm*. Our mid-week truancy is propelled by the dark, brooding spiritedness of "Tempus Fugit," a tune devised by J.J. Johnson and recorded by Miles for Blue Note. We've been playing that little ten-inch LP until the groves are white from needle wear. It's hip and we know it, for in our amusement park minds we are hipness personified.

We've picked up on all the stories our heroes were telling

on this album, even though words have nothing to do with it, and as sly adolescents given to analyzing the world note by note and look by look we're shot through with visions of the adult world as a hall of mirrors where nothing is as it appears to be.

In my own head, that world is dark, the color of a blood-red rose, a fragile flower that everybody seems to want to trample when they aren't busy stepping on one another's toes. Yet sunning itself in this garden of suspicion is the tender conviction that jazz, true jazz dedication and devotion, means being addicted to something. We're all on that wavelength, thinking that way; feeling anyway. Dumb and tender, we figure the addiction's got to be physical rather than mental or spiritual. We haven't yet learned that music is really all about ourselves.

And so off to the movies we rush to see how Sinatra portrays a junkie, the on-screen version of a heroin addict. We aren't so dumb as to not know that bebop and getting high went hand in hand somehow, even though we ourselves aren't addicted to anything yet, not even the beer and whiskey and occasional reefer that comes our way from time to time.

The time we do our hardest listening is afternoon; two-story-flat, after-school afternoons spent in the diningroom, kitchen and livingroom of Don's and Al's parents' home on Gladstone Street. Sometimes we sneak shots of whiskey from their gym teacher father's Jim Beam or Seagram's Seven Crown bottles. Or, because I look older than my actual age, they'll paint a mustache on me and send me out to score jumbo quarts of Pfeiffer's or, better yet, Stroh's Bohemian beer. Then, with our senses systematically deranged for the moment, we kick back and get off into this swaggering, athletic, cultish music that speaks directly to the rebellious side of our delicate natures, the side that's determined to give the finger to the world and remain cool, be cool, be.

We jazzed June, and then some! Hey, man, just leave us be.

Bebop? That's what they've named it but, strictly speaking, the music's got no name. At the time bebop, to me anyway, is something else—cute and pat; the kind of sounds that cascaded in diminished and augmented chromatic runs along New York's 52nd Street with bee-stings of heroin lubricating knuckles and embouchures and the snappy feet and wrists of skinny drummers just waiting for the chance to call themselves percussionists. No, this isn't bebop; not Miles's music with titles like "Kilo," "Lazy Susan," and "Tempus Fugit."

We've sought and have been granted asylum in the school band where—with other wearers of coal-black, horn-rimmed shades and Stetson shoes—we pour our tough little hearts and souls into our instruments, sneering at the bogus authority of home, parents, school authority and everything familiar, established and therefore suspect. In darkest adolescence, we brood our way through corny marches and stock pop charts, waiting for a chance to slip our hip licks in and blow away the band instructor and the uninitiated among us.

In the poolroom when somebody says, "I ain't seen you since I don't know when," the proper, studied rejoinder is: "Well, you know how it is—*tempus* sure do *fugit*, don't it?"

And Don, who was truly comic back there in the heyday of Mack Man style, can stand in front of the poolroom across from the butcher's, fingering the brim of his stingybrim hat, puffing on a Chesterfield, going: "Uh, since I can't go to Birdland and hear me no sounds, I guess I'll walk over here to Meat Land and get me some meat."

It makes no more sense now than it did then, but the music still glues it all together like a vaudeville routine that's never been given the hook.

FOUR, 1955

Don't ask me how come, but suddenly it's high spring and

the trees are all too much for me to take in their urban beauty and blossoming headiness. I'm sappy, I'm happy, I'm happening in a way that makes me want to serve notice that I'm subject to fly clean out of my body at any moment and stand still in the sky overlooking it all, a crazy-faced hummingbird of spirit, drunk on sonic nectar. Relaxed and ripening, I've got the perfect set of sounds to go with what I'm feeling; got Blakey, got Percy, got Horace Silver, got Miles, got Miles, got Miles to go.

"Four" is the name of the tune, all right, but four what? For now it don't matter. For now I'm in love the way you're generically in love when you're 16 and gone. In love, with what? A girl? Yes. Which one? All girls.

But mainly it's this bubbling sense of late April ebullience that floats me along the shores of the Detroit River, West Grand Boulevard, Dexter Avenue, Palmer Park and 12th Street. Please don't ask me to explain anything; it's all being said on the record by Miles and them everytime I put it on and take it off there's a different way they're saying the same thing which is what I remember when I play it back in my head too and all it is is the only message I've ever wanted to hear going way back into my deepest self that sings and sails saying be happy love is all there is O can't you feel it pulling you through the thaw of this frozen street the world into melting warm waves of the fragrant heaven you've been reaching for for so long?

Later, but not much later, along came singing poet Jon Hendricks with Dave Lambert and Annie Ross to sound it all out in crisp, zigzag vocalese, citing truth, honor, happiness and love as the four components essential to full living; putting words to all the solos. It was a marvelous interpretation—true to Miles's and the other on-the-spot composers' every note and nuance—only something got lost.

Music's like that; it comes already translated, ready to be understood by anyone with ears. What I was hearing you already know, but don't bank on it; there's too much beforeness and afterness clouding our telepathy.

All you need to know is the name of the song is "Four," and no more.

TUNE UP, 1955

The power of music is such that you'll find yourself wallowing on the ground or floor of it on your way to eternity.

And what is eternity but a vibration; the same stuff we're made of—vibrations—"I ain't got no body," being the musical truth of it. The love, the kiss, the hug and sock and wham of it in doubles and triples is sugar still; the I-love-you rushing through these hard knocks and fists pounding in the sand of love; the soft let's do it again and again of wet lips and eyes and muscles.

There are ways to say this in French, Tagalog, Japanese and Maori, or in jazz. But I love you is all anybody can ever say by way of commitment and surrender to Life, the Infinite, Divine Intelligence, the only real Lover; the force to which the higher self is always tuned whether you can hear it or not.

It's only the look of things that gets in the way; that is, until you tune up and remember there's no such thing as "I Got Rhythm"; you are rhythm. And how could you ever let a song go out of your heart, when you are already song?

O the beautiful changes!

BLUES FOR PABLO, 1957

And who was Pablo? What did it mean? Pablo Casals? Pablo Picasso? Now, why would Miles Davis and Gil Evans be doing a blues for Pablo Picasso? On the other hand, why not? Hadn't Picasso come into his own, and somehow hadn't he—in spirit perhaps or by way of Matisse—gotten himself connected up with jazz?

Even I had grown up on those old fanciful, inky David Stone Martin illustrations of musicians in their shoes and hats and instruments embellished with curlycue stitches all artsy and modern like the packaging of jazz for the connoisseur you were for sure when you kicked down two weeks of lunch money for one of Norman Granz's glossy *Jazz at the Philharmonic* 33-1/3 long-playing microgroove recordings.

David Stone Martin was a disciple of the illustrious Ben Shahn, a painter whose political consciousness and leanings had grown dangerously unfashionable by then, the days of Pat Boone, Patti Page, Eddie Fisher and The Four Aces. It was black Detroit artist Harold Neal, one of my early mentors, who'd mentioned to me more than once how Shahn, a WPA survivor of the Great Depression, was said to have stayed up nights wielding a broken matchstick tip to achieve that jagged line and the intense effect that made his drawings and his imitators famous. Whether this is true or not no longer matters stylistically, but I've always associated Shahn with Pablo Picasso, that master of art trend consciousness. And when the subject of Picasso comes up, I'm mindful that the world's foremost collector of Picasso's work for years and years was jazz producer Norman Granz who, after abandoning the States to take up residence in Switzerland, even named his record label after the exiled Spaniard. Pablo Records has long been one of the most commercially successful of independent jazz labels.

But labels are one thing and substance another. I've imparted all this to indicate how eager I'd been at one time to pin down a title. Why that seemed important is now inexplicable. What matters is that *Miles Ahead* was the first long playing album I'd ever heard with no silence separating its selections. One track gracefully segued into another. Later this kind of production came to be known in the industry as a "concept" album. It was Gil Evans's subtle yet intricate orchestral arrangements and Miles's cool-to-warm-to-torrid blowing that kept my blood simmering. It was the dressing up of the humble old irreducible blues form and the fresh-sounding modernity and paint job these artists had given it that startled. In fact, there was something so vital about this process of transformation, this blues-primed paint job, that "Blues for Pablo" still sounds as vivid and dewy today as it always did. Seductive—that's the word. "Blues for Pablo" sounds painted; sounds as if it's been painted right onto some invisible sound-conducting substance.

Ahead of myself, I'd walk around Ann Arbor when the season was nose-stiffening cold, then repair to my East William Street digs, the house with the bay window overlooking Maynard Street, slip on this record and thaw out until my blue-brown nostrils were wide open. Sometimes I wonder who I thought I was then. What was all that craziness I seem to have made up about warming myself on January nights to mellowing sounds? What was it about those sounds—Miles's and Evans's versions of Brubeck's "The Duke" or Ahmad Jamal's "New Rhumba" or "Blues for Pablo"—that made me long to be walking around Central Park along the Manzanares River in Madrid or the Champs Elysées in early-blooming May?

BLUE IN GREEN, 1958

What you hear is what you are.

If rain is pouring out of Coltrane's horn and Cannonball Adderley and Bill Evans and Paul Chambers and Jimmy Cobb are floating beneath it bearing rainbowed umbrellas, that's because the melody you need loves a showered floor to move it along the way ocean needs sand.

The beached house your mind occupies now is only just that; a dwelling-place for now, for now. The pain you're feeling—played back to you as mischievous joy—is all you require to usher you out of this moment.

Put yourself on a boat going nowhere. Where does your journey end or begin?

Were you even born when this record first came out? Did you smooch to it like I did, clinging to behold the fundamental need and pleasure of physical affection and to be held? Did it make your scalp tingle the first time you heard it? Can you point out the lovers on ths crossing in watery off-shore waltz time; the ones you knowingly sailed around or steered clear of, and which ones finally sneaked up and gotcha?

There are smooth or rocky transitions into or away from everything imaginable. Each gradation of approach has a color, and every color a name to be sounded—from prismatic blue to greasy green—and the distances we're talking about exist in mind, not time, and mind alone.

Consider fauna and flora and grit beneath water being pulled by beams of tightly packed light: a common kind of blue.

ALL BLUES, 1958

When, as a kid, I first heard the blues—heard them, that is, and paid attention to what I was hearing—I recognized their special quality at once. I understood exactly what they were. An instantaneous connection was made.

Perhaps if you'd come at me and asked me to explain, I would've been tongue-tied, yet all the feelings were there, all the deep and scattered and complex emotions, even at the age of four. I can still conjure those feelings up today with all the intensity of sunlight directed through the lens of a magnifying glass; the magnifying glass me and my playmates used to roast ants to a crisp in the front and back yards of our ignorance.

Looking back, it's easy to see now how Mississippi wasn't

a bad place to get initiated into the blues. It was all around us. I understood instantly what the blues meant, and that understanding had nothing to do with analysis or quantification; flatted thirds and fifths and sevenths or twelve or sixteen bars or tonal centers or the history of human oppression or class struggle. To paraphrase something the late Big Bill Broonzy once said off the cuff, you were simply living with the blues if you came up in the South around the time I was coming along.

The blues and I caught back up with each other in Jackson, Mississippi a few years ago when I was checking into the Hilton Hotel there as part of a gig Margaret Walker, author of the novel *Jubilee*, had put together at the University. It was one of those afternoons when the veritable shadow of Reconstruction, so to speak, was in effect. All the desk clerks and switchboard operators, just then anyway, were black, and all the bellboys white.

The gnarly lad who toted and carted my luggage up to the fifth floor was carrying on a flipflop conversation with me. His attention seemed to have perked up when I mentioned I was from Mississippi. He poked his doorkey in the lock of the room that was supposed to be mine, pushed until a chain lock blocked further entry, then started cussing. Then, while I waited, he descended by elevator to consult with the desk man. After that we went up to the fifth floor, tried another door and found that it too was already occupied. Down he went again and came back up with yet another key. When we finally got into a room that seemed free for me to move into, he grimly performed his bellboy duties—hauling my bags in, snapping on the lights, and so on—then waited patiently for his tip.

But once the buck had been snugly pocketed, he blinked at me quizzically and, turning to leave, said, "How long you say you lived in Mississippi?"

"Spent pretty much most of my first ten years here."

"Well," he said, scratching his sandy hair, "look like to

me you'da been smart enough to get outta this state a helluva lot sooner. Anyway, welcome home. I reckon you can see ain't too much done changed."

Certainly, the blues haven't changed; they never do at heart. The feelings I experienced the first time I lay in bed listening to Cab Calloway or Johnny Mercer singing "Blues in the Night" from the radio nextdoor in my parents' bedroom weren't much different from what I felt when Miles's unbelievably beautiful "All Blues," served up in deliciously brisk 3/4 waltz time, got ahold of me the way the train along the tracks across the street used to do in Ocean Springs when it rumbled past in the night with its lonesome whistle moaning: *Oooooweeee!* "My mama done told me . . ."

The album *Kind of Blue*, I'm told, was more pianist Bill Evans's conception than Miles's, but what does it matter now that all these eerie years have sprung up around whatever plot first seeded it? Physicists will tell you that the color blue absorbs red, orange, and yellow rays at the same time that it radiates green, violet, indigo and its own stately hue. And having been haunted by "All Blues" these many years, I can tell you there's no way to even begin quantifying the infinite qualities of blueness.

Sky blue, ocean blue, lake blue, ice blue, blood blue, vein blue, neon blue, flame blue, periwinkle blue, steely blue, nipple blue, royal blue, true blue, moon blue, midnight blue, mountain blue, snow blue, powder blue, algae blue, devil blue, heavenly blue, blossom blue, Nile blue, stocking blue, moldy blue, radiant blue, electric blue, shadow blue, twilight blue, navy blue, star blue, movie blue, misty blue, ribbon blue, fox blue, feather blue, and on and on into the blueness of your very essence—not even to mention exclusively human kinds of blue.

No, I didn't think I'd ever get over these blues; not until I woke up one night in the middle of a troubling dream and it hit me there was a realm beyond the blues, reds, oranges, yellows and all the rest of the spectrum. That was where I needed to be; brilliantly blended back in with the dazzling iridescence of the very force that powers life itself. That's all. That was all the blues had taught me and all I needed to learn from years of living with the blues, the whole blues and nothing but the blues.

SKETCHES OF SPAIN, 1960

Wandering around Madrid in the early Sixties, I saw Gil Evans's gorgeous orchestrations being acted out, with Miles's inspired trumpet blowing like a coastal wind above it all. I wove it into the Spain I'd dragged to Spain with me, a Spain I had in fact invented from Don Quijote, Sancho Panza, Lorca's *Gypsy Ballads,* flamenco music and dance, images of solemn yet lovely Andalusian women in lace mantillas, the Cartheginians, the Romans, the Moors, the Inquisition, expulsion of the Semites in 1492, *El Siglo de Oro* (the so-called Golden Age of empire and culture), Goya's paintings, Unamuno's *Tragic Sense of Life,* philosopher Santayana's essays on solipsism, the films of Luis Bunuel, Salvador Dali's brand of surrealism, the Spanish Civil War, the Communist and loyalist activist known as La Pasionaria, Generalisimo Francisco Franco, fascism, persecution, Lorca's unexplained assassination, Picasso's *Guérnica* and folksong piled atop folksong (Hello, Germaine Montero!) in the part of my head that warehoused such things.

I figured nobody on the Iberian Peninsula had ever heard of Miles Davis or American jazz, and yet one rainy night, stopping by a little bar in a workingclass section of town, I stood by the jukebox with a tall, cheap rum and coke in hand, and punched up Louis Armstrong's version of the African song "Skokian" along with Cozy Cole's old hit "Topsy: Part Two." The instant the music began drenching the little joint with warmth, I looked up to see a table of young black men who'd been sizing me up. Suddenly they were nudging each other and flashing friendly smiles. They motioned for me to join them. Their seeming leader, cheerful and in his early twenties, told me in Spanish: "When you played the right stuff on the box we knew you had to be one of us!"

They were Africans from Spanish Guinea who were studying in Madrid, some of them air force officers. They opened up completely to me and accepted me into their fold. We'd get together afternoons, and sometimes at night, to discuss everything under the sun except politics. Oh, they let me know in so many words that they were hip to the colonial scheme of things but that the wheel of history was still turning and turning, don't you see? Philosophy they loved and were well versed in the classical version of it. But that didn't stop them from being themselves nor from pausing between salient points in our chats to playfully firm up some assignation or rendezvous with one or another of the frisky Spanish women who either worked the place or worked in it as barmaids or waitresses. I perceived that the cat-and-mouse game of life goes on all the same under repressive or permissive regimes.

They told me about Africa. I told them about the States. I told them about Miles Davis and *Sketches of Spain*. They asked if I'd like to act in a movie some Cuban woman was making about the people of color in Madrid, and would I like to come to dinner sometime? I felt funny about both invitations because I was poor and living in a ridiculously cheap room at the Pensión Galápagos on the wrong side of the Gran Via. I simply didn't think I'd be able to reciprocate their hospitality, and so I never took them up on it. I chose instead to limit our relationship to a bar/cafe setting. I thought of us as latter-day Moors; they saw all black people the world over as an oppressed but gifted race with a special contribution to make to mankind.

It was all so singularly beautiful and warm that—even

now, having dissolved from the third into the fifth decade of my quiet residence on earth—the lush and breathing strains of *Sketches of Spain* are enough to send me meandering through the streets and rooms and rest stops of an ancient Madrid that's probably only the product of an unhurried stroll I took once through a Prado Museum of the mind.

FEVER
Little Willie John, 1956
&
OOH POO PAH DOO
Jesse Hill, 1960

The deal was you worked eight to twelve hours a day, beginning at four in the afternoon and quitting whenever you were told to go home. This was at the docks, as they were called, down on Seventh Street in Oakland, California, and it was the whipping winter of 1964.

I had passed the so-called exam which required, as I recall, that you kneel before a snickering examiner and hoist a one-hundred-pound sack to your shoulder and stand back up without buckling in his presence.

"Congratulations!" the chipper man told me. "You're a mail handler now. Report to work on Monday."

And so began three months of working for the U.S. Postal Service again, only this time it was as one of society's mules rather than as a clerk. Our job was to tackle and drag sacks of mail off the loading docks and stack them into the trucks backed up there. I never ached so much in my life.

We worked in teams of eight to ten, and there were two supervisors: a stocky gent named Jones who was brown-skinned and jovial, and a giant named Brown whom I prefer to call Red because of his light, freckled, reddish complexion and also because he was something of a devil. Jones, who ate a lot on the job, wore a greasy work jacket and a felt hat with the brim upturned. Anytime the sandwich man wheeled by, Jones flagged him down and grabbed himself a po'boy or a pie or something. I was skinny then but I liked to do that too, never suspecting, not until somebody pulled my coat weeks later that I'd become a favorite of Jones because he liked a man who liked to eat.

Red was altogether something else. He came on duty around eight at night when Jones punched out, and he came on hungry and mean. Red carried around with him an old newspaper clipping preserved in plastic that told of the time shortly following the Korean War when he'd broken the record for a mail handler by working something like six months in a row, with no days off, for twelve full hours a day. The Postal Service had apparently seen fit to give this workaholic a salutory citation instead of telling that such a performance was actually threatening his health and well-being. He was made to see himself as a hero when he should've been reprimanded. Call it capitalism, call it socialism, call it the work ethic, call it whatever you want. I called it one sad day the night I locked horns with the Old Red Devil.

It was well known to everybody that worked on the docks but me that you didn't so much as whisper to Red when he was having his lunch. Lunch for Red took place at ten every night, and his passion was gumbo. He could probably consume it by the bucket, but he had to settle for two nightly quarts of the stuff which was served up by a joint closeby known as Esther's—a rhythm and blues bar and lounge that also specialized in barbecued ribs, chicken, chitlins, greens, gumbo, and all the usual soulfood.

Little Willie John was hanging out after hours in Esther's in those days, but he was on his last legs, having fallen on the proverbial evil days. No longer the perky, churchy-throated kid who had written and recorded the hit tune "Fever" in his teens, Little Willie was tired now and seemed a little lost. He'd turn up at Esther's to drink and goof and cut the fool; a superlative artist, still in need of more than the two, maybe three hits he'd enjoyed, and frustrated, I suspect, in an all-too-soon kind of way. There's no telling what might've been rushing and curdling around inside Willie John by then. Not long afterwards I happened to catch him as the opening act at a Jackie "Moms" Mabley show at the Oakland Auditorium, but in no time he'd killed a man and landed in the state penitentiary up in Washington where he died. Details, as they usually are in such situations, are blurred. What isn't blurred are my memories of him being there at the peripheries of that short-lasting gig situated in the depths of Oakland, in the heart of what later came to be romantically known as the ghetto.

Believe me, there was nothing at all romantic about it. Sometimes, waiting for the last bus home in the very entrails of darkness, I'd be watching patterns my frosty breath made in the icy night air, then look up and catch a tableaux being played out across the street involving some hooker who'd been accosted or mistreated by some john. Suddenly her pimp and some buddies would appear on the scene and smash the shit out of the offender before my eyes. The funky bus would pull up and I would board, still trying to absorb what I'd just seen. The bus would roll away. I'd go home and dream tired, uninspired dreams.

Red had his rules. I broke one of them without knowing about it until it was too late.

One night when he was meditatively slurping gumbo with a plastic spoon, I tapped at the partly opened door of Red's hideaway room. All I wanted was to ask if it was OK to take a break. Red was sitting with his back halfway turned to me in the half-dark. From a glance I could tell that eating was a religious ritual with Red. Hunched over his gumbo in that checkered, tattered plaid woolen hunting coat and baseball cap, his eyes, half-closed behind steamy glasses, rolled my way with a tilt of his head. I saw the scowl on his face, but that scowl was Red's natural expression. When he wasn't scowling, his leathery face wavered between a totally deadpan expression and a slow-burn. Red was one miserable specimen of *homo afro-americanus.*

Just as I was about to knock again, still very much the innocent bystander, one of the guys from the crew, an ex-boxer named Brick, just happened to be stomping down the narrow hallway. In a flash, Brick sized up the situation, grabbed me by the elbow and dragged me along with him until we'd reached a spot that was safely out of Red's earshot.

"Young," he said in a gruff whisper, "you lost your mind?"

"What're you talking about?"

"I mean, I know you one of them Ninety-Day-Wonders, but you bout to get your block knocked clean off."

"Hey, Jones kept me working through my break when he went off-shift and I needed to ask Red if—"

Brick had a way of flailing his arms and wrists about, as if he might be loosening up for a sparring session or something, and he did this vigorously as he explained: "I don't care what the hell you need to ask. Ain't nobody told you don't be fuckin with Red when he greazin?"

"But all I did was knock! I wasn't about to get him in no big conversation."

"Man, what you was *about* to do was rile Red up and get him mad!"

"Mad about what?"

"Listen, you must don't know so I'mo try to tell you. Whenever you see food in fronta Red and he gettin ready to chow down or even if it's just him and cupa coffee and he be off by hisself, you don't say boo to him!"

"What's the matter with him?"

"What's the matter with him? Hell, I ain't no psychiatrist but I do know this much—the nigger crazy and he just might get it in his head to kill you."

"You jivin."

"All right, you think I'm jivin, you walk on back there

and knock on that door one more time. We'll read about it in the *Tribune*—'Champion Muthafukkin Dock Foreman Go Berserk and Waste Ninety-Day-Wonder!' "

"You *are* serious, aren't you?"

"Serious as a heart attack, Jack! You stick around here and last out your few weeks, you gon know about Red when they spring your educated ass loose! I done saved you this time, but you better put some kinda restraint on yourself next time you go pullin that shit!"

There was no next time. Innocent though I often was on this job, I was fast at catching on once I'd pieced a sticky situation together. It became perfectly obvious that what the veteran dockers said about Red was true. But I did manage to run rather seriously afoul of another one of Red's unwritten rules. Put into language, it would probably run something like this: *Pull anything you wanna pull, just don't let me catch you at it.*

As Christmas grew closer and closer and the mails heated up to the point where it was all we mail handlers could do to help slide the sacks down the roller conveyors and chunk and heave them onto the trucks, everyone began working so many extra hours that at any given time we were punchy and wiped. While others worked and kept watch, one or the other crew guys were given to taking naps on those sacks that were deepest inside the trucks. This was common stuff. Jones knew about it, and I imagine all the other supervisors did. After all, this was the Post Office which, in those days, had its own peculiar friendship and kinship network, to say nothing of the curious manner in which it was managed. It wasn't at all unusual, for example, for a particular male worker to be shifted into a new slot and for his on-the-job girlfriend to be shifted at the same time or, in any case, shortly thereafter. These people looked out for one another.

Then, too, you've got to remember that the scene was predominantly black, and not just black but invisibly divided up into native territories. There were Texans,

Louisianans, Arkies, Okies, Northerners, born-Californians, and so forth. It got even tinier than that: Among the Louisiana Negroes alone, there was an intense and muttering rivalry between New Orleans, Baton Rouge, Lafayette, Shreveport and St. Charles Negroes. "Them niggers outta St. Charles," Brick might grumble, "they think they the slickest niggers in the world and don't nobody else know nothin!" Or you might hear a native St. Charlesean such as the olive-skinned, straight-haired Handsome Tony say, "The average muthafukka you see workin here couldn't make it in St. Charles cause they got the I.Q. of a bunion." And that pretty much told you the score.

On one of those nights I happened to be the one copping a few Z's atop the more recondite truck cargo. It seems I'd begun my snooze while Jones was on duty. As a matter of fact, I'd dozed off thinking about how much Jones reminded me of that old album organist Jimmy Smith and guitarist Wes Montgomery teamed up on; the one with a jacket photograph that shows them face to face, practically nose to nose, munching on twin hero or po'boy sandwiches. Somebody's transistor radio was blatting out Jesse Hill's "Ooh Poo Pah Doo," one of the biggies on KDIA, the black music AM radio station that called itself Lucky 13. And from here to eternity, "Ooh Poo Pah Doo" will always conjure back up what happened that night.

Red, who had evidently moved the crew from my nap truck to work another one down the dock, clunked up inside the truck in his John Henry workshoes, spotted me snoring there and started screaming at the top of his voice: "Well, well, what do we have here? Nigger! Nigger, get your ass up from there this minute! I said get the fuck up! Who the hell you think you are anyway? Get up and get outta this truck!"

I got up at once and got out. Red, in all his not-to-be-believed ugliness, was trembling as he smacked the fist of one hand into the palm of the other. "Young," he said, "you know I done just about had it with you! I want you to get your ass over to Special Packages. You gonna be workin with Cowboy for the resta the night!"

And that's where I went. Cowboy was an oldtimer on the docks; a lean, jeaned, workshirted man who sported dark glasses, a vest, a wiry full beard and a chewed up, ridiculous cowboy hat. He didn't talk much and he worked you hard and fast. But I could tell he had a sense of humor buried someplace beneath that blind exterior of his. If Red gave off a junkyard dog vibration, Cowboy's was more like that of the silent wreckingyard hand whose job it was to reach into the bowels of some not quite totally cannibalized auto and tear out, say, or a pair of heater boxes from an old Volkswagen Bug. And whenever Cowboy would strut along the docks on his way to lunch or on a break, regulars would inevitably turn to one another and say, "Yon go Cowboy. Go on, Cowboy, with your crazy, bad self!"

Cowboy and I got along just fine. I did what he instructed me to do and, from time to time, he'd give me one of those paternal smiles that meant everything was in order and moving right along. Red was off in Hothead Heaven and Cowboy was rounding up everything that needed to be fed into the grander and more practical scheme of things.

Eventually I was brought back to work with my old crew, but Red, I noticed, left me alone. I couldn't figure out why until Brick told me one night what had taken place the Sunday I'd chosen to stay home.

"You missed it, Young, you missed it!" he said gleefully.

"Missed what?"

"The night you was home, Red come in here all worked up and went to gettin on Cowboy's case. Now, Cowboy, mind you, he just as ignorant and ready to die as Red, only he don't make no big thing outta that. So Red jumped off up in Cowboy's chest bout some bullshit that wasn't none of Red's business in the first place and Cowboy he give Red one of them smiles of his—you know that grin—and when Red wouldn't take the hint and back off like somebody with some sense Old Cowboy pulled a pistol on the nigger and you know what Red did?"

"What?"

"Red punched out, that's what!"

"Hunh?"

"That's right, Red who spose to be so bad and ready, he throwed up them hamhock handsa his and punched out, that's what he did! See, Red wasn't thinkin bout meetin his match. See, it's bad niggers and it's quiet niggers and sometimes it's hard to tell which is which."

I let go of the sack I'd been lugging when Brick told me that; let go of it and laughed in the shadows of the truck, thinking about the way Jesse Hill had been shouting over the dock radios all fall about how he was going to "ring a few bells in your ears" and how he wasn't going to stop trying until he could create "confusion in your mind."

My ears were ringing, my mind was messed up and, having become a zombie who got home in the very wee hours to scrawl out a note for his nine-to-five working wife, I was aching to move out of all the Red zones of the world and innocently into the ever-elusive green.

I GOT RHYTHM

George Gershwin, composer

Imagine, if you can, endless chorses of "I Got Rhythm" stretched out back to back with seductive, bludgeoning blues from the 1920s clean into the very next century, and there you got it, man, there you got this thing called jazz squirming by the scruff of its neck stretched out far enough to reach anywhere, far enough to poke its warm, wet nose smugly into the snuggest corners of the world with a grin that can either end or begin just about anyplace you want it to.

Say, what?

Say, there's absolutely no telling where this stuff'll put you if you let it. My mama used to say, "All that crazy music, it's gon drive you crazy you aint careful!" And she was right. But I was careful. Bluesman Jimmy Reed say, "All them musicians played that bebop, they all either ended up dyin early or else they went insane." And he was right too. No getting around it. Look at the record. Listen to it close. Think about all the people with ears unchecked in love with this dangerous music who wound up on dope or unable to get up in the morning; humans who married outside their race or lost their place in line at the Supermarket of Life. Think about people whose inner ear led them to the far edges of Earth and inner space. Think about vast, cosmic surges of blues pouring down over your hot, troubled soul like a worldly, liquidy balm of tropical rain whose spiritual cousin is that same old sun the Aztecs and Egyptians knowingly worshipped.

When Mr. George Gershwin sat down and knocked out "I Got Rhythm," did he have any idea what the Negroes and the Negrophiles would do with it; how they would dress it up and mess with it and test it to its outer limits? Never mind the Negrophobes. That sound crept in and got to them too, even those among them who later had the nerve to ponder and cogitate the dire prospect that there might not would've even been such a music had it not been for the brilliant compositional efforts of this Jewish gentleman named Gershwin.

Well, let's face it, the thoroughly lovable Mr. Gershwin had plenty sense, enough to go directly to the source: to the Negroes, that is, for inspiration. No Negroes, no "I Got Rhythm." No Negroes, no American music. No Negroes, no America. No America, no jazz. And that's just for openers.

Even Dr. Joseph Goebbels, Hitler's Minister of Propaganda—an unsuccessful novelist, playwright and liberal journalist—had enough insight to observe in what remains of his diaries: "... The Americans have the ability of taking their relatively small stock of culture and by a modernized version to make of it something very à propos for the present time ... The Americans have only a few Negro songs, but they present them in such a modern way that they conquer large parts of the modern world which is, of course, very fond of such melodies. We have a much greater fund of cultural goods, but we have neither the artistry nor the will to modernize them. That will have to be changed."*

But if it's true that much of the Nazi high command turned to heroin, morphine, cocaine and other heavy drugs when dark days came toward the end of the War, you wonder what might've happened had they given jazz and peace a chance. You wonder.

Imagine, if you can, endless choruses of this sprightly 32-bar tune, "I Got Rhythm," probed by some of the world's finest musicians; the Master Race presided over by His Master's Voice.

Imagine it all being transformed into something else again and again and again.

The Goebbels Diaries, 1942-43; edited, translated and with an introduction by Louis P. Lochner; Doubleday & Company, Inc., New York, 1948.

THE POETRY MAN

Phoebe Snow, 1975

My first really liberating experience as a teacher of writing happened in the winter of 1967. Ronald Dahl, the noted Bay Area artist, was conducting a series of Saturday afternoon art classes at the San Francisco Museum of Art under the auspices of the Museum's Teen Workshop Program. Ron, whose talents and interests extend to filmmaking and poetry-writing, asked if I'd be interested in coming and speaking to the class about poetry in particular and about writing in general. A number of his workshop students had expressed interest in experimenting with linguistic as well as graphic and pictorial idiom. I could come by regularly for a few weeks and we'd see how it worked out. At the time, the thought of trying to teach any form of creative writing, especially to young people, put me on edge, but, charged with curiosity, I said OK, that I'd be willing to try my hand at it but on a purely tentative basis.

Six Saturdays later, I found that I had fallen in love with the whole workshop idea. Just how much help I had been to students as a writing instructor during that period would be hard to say. I doubt if any teacher, particularly one working the area loosely termed Arts & Humanities, ever really knows if he's getting anything at all across to a class. Besides, I'd always known somehow that writing couldn't be taught. You could teach literature. You could teach a certain kind of "appreciation." You could teach rules of grammar, punctuation, effective syntax—any of the peripheral elements essential to most kinds of writing. You could teach descriptive writing, i.e., the writing of essays, journalistic accounts, editorials, business letters, and so on. But when it came right down to the nitty-gritty, the art of writing imaginatively and well was something that couldn't be taught.

Like most writers who've been to college, I'd sat through my share of creative writing courses and seminars. My best teacher had been the late Allan Seager, novelist and author of *The Glass House* (a personalized biography of the poet Theodore Roethke), at the University of Michigan. Seager would sit up in class and charm all of us with his formidable repertoire of anecdotes; personal reminiscences of his own early writing and magazine-editing days, stories about other writers he had known, and just generally rap on and on about himself, books, publishers, madmen and the exigencies of writing as a career. He was a superb storyteller and his classes were quite popular. In his office, however, he talked with you about your work, giving sound and compassionate advice. His conversation was instructional. In my senior year, for example, he finished reading a long piece that I'd typed on teletype paper à la Jack Kerouac about hitching cross country with just a guitar and a couple of pairs of socks, and advised me to hurry up and get the hell out of school and go live in the world but to keep writing. We could talk to one another. This is why I remember him as being an important teacher. The fact that we could communicate meant so much.

What I had fallen in love with during those early awkward attempts of mine to teach writing at the SF Museum was the experience of being around people younger than myself in a way that felt meaningful. Between 1967 and 1969 I had the pleasure of conducting a number of poetry and writing workshops for both the Museum and the Berkeley/Oakland Neighborhood Youth Corps, bringing me into contact with students from a variety of cultural and economic backgrounds, ranging in age from 11 through 17. It was during this period that I found out something that I'd suspected all along: most public school education is deathly in the way that it stifles creativity.

Imagination is a dirty word in our educational setup. By the time most kids enter college, the growth of their imaginative faculties has been seriously stunted from disuse. The damage has been done. Either you've gone along with the program and molded yourself to the standards and requirements (which is to say: limitations) of the system, content to get good enough grades to get to college and then into some grad school, or you've dropped out. Increasingly the numbers of brighter youngsters, unable to cope with the emptiness and meaninglessness, are simply dropping out.

Why is that? Why should a 12-year-old be apt to put more life and spontaneity into the writing of a poem, say, than the average English major? Why do we marvel at books such as June Meyer Jordan's *Voices of the Children,* Richard Lewis' *Miracles,* and Kenneth Koch's *Lies, Wishes and Dreams?* I believe it's because most of us, as adults and even as parents or teachers, are sadly ignorant of the kind of creative and imaginative energy that children are capable of harnessing and generating. Collections of children's writings, such as those I've mentioned, by going beyond the cute Art Linkletter "Kids-Say-the-Darndest Things" format, remind us of our own creative potential which, in most people, lies dormant, undeveloped, and therefore untapped.

Poet Diane Wakoski says that she hates children's art. "There's something phoney about it." She hates the way it's dished up commercially for adults to nibble at. Robert Oppenheimer, on the other hand, was fond of saying that there were children playing in the streets capable of assisting him in the solution of some of his most difficult problems involving higher physics and mathematics largely because they still had access to intuitional and imaginational modes of perception and thinking that had gradually become closed off to him as a well-trained adult scientist. I suppose, in a sense, that children live poetry all day long. It's no secret that as we grow and make all the adjustments required of us for functioning in society, we also run the risk of losing much of our day-to-day soulfulness. Soul, as I use it here, refers not so much to a thing as it does to a way in which things happen, to paraphrase Faraday's classic description of electricity. It's a quality, a force, if you will, the presence of which forces us to distinguish between such concepts as *man* and *human.* The difference is more than a matter of *hue;* it's a matter of *you.* Children and most other people who haven't been overly processed or programmed or repressed have soul. Kenneth Patchen, in *The Journal of Albion Moonlight,* says "that as far as growing up is concerned, most men grow down." If most of us were trained from childhood to keep in touch with our basic selves and to develop the use of our intuitions to serve us less destructively, encounter groups, gestalt therapy, touch sensitivity training, psychodrama and all the rest of it would be utterly unnecessary.

How did I go about "teaching" writing to 6th through 12th graders? To be truthful, I didn't so much teach as put myself in the middle of it all, attempting to function as catalytic agent, someone who set the stage for things to take place. I tried to create an atmosphere in which student efforts would be taken seriously. I tried to share some of the things that I had learned about imaginative writing as a person who'd been working at it since childhood. However, anytime I came on too pedantic or self-consciously pedagogical, someone was sure to call me on it. "I thought you told us this wasn't going to be like school!" The only way I could keep participants in both the Museum and the NYC workshops attending on a voluntary basis was by promising them that it wasn't going to be like school.

"I think I got a few things to say," a paranoid young man told me one afternoon, "but, like, the teachers at school don't ever really give you a chance to just blow, you know what I mean? Like, the kinda jive they be tryna get you to write just don't be all that interesting to me, the way they teach it, you know. I just think it's nice to blow soul every once in a while, just do your own thing, tell what's on your own mind." This same young man, once freed from his fear of not being able to spell or use grammar or punctuate properly, produced a number of poems and deeply-felt personal statements in prose that really got to everybody in the workshop. ". . . Man in search of time/but lost in his own self, so lost he can't be found,/wandering from place to place with noplace to go./ . . . Man with his dice and guns and wars/is the most hateful being in the universe./Why? Why must there be/this unending/bloodshed, like a giant web that catches every/one and everything in it?/ . . . in a world where there could be so much/love/instead of the pain and hate on the faces around you./That's right, look at your friends unsuspected,/do you see the unsure look on their faces?/Why?" L.K. Wallace (the initials don't stand for anything) wrote this after studing an abstract pattern projected on a wall during a light show put on for the workshop by members of the now-defunct Pegasus Project, a revolving assemblage of young poets who recited and performed in classrooms and school auditoriums around the Bay Area in the late 1960s.

Each group of students I worked with produced a magazine, a mimeographed or, in some instances, offset-reproduced anthology of workshop writings. Participants shared the duties of selection, editing, typing, illustrating, collating, stapling and distribution. I usually felt happy just being in on the excitement. It was so good to be working outside the confines of the official educational system. "If only this kind of interaction could be achieved in public schools! What a difference it would make!" There'd be times when I'd show up for a session with no particular plan in mind for that day. Many of the best meetings happened under those circumstances. Things would start popping the minute I got inside the room and it would be touch and go for the next couple of hours. I came to the conclusion that a teacher can do both his class and himself a disfavor by always turning up overly prepared. The lesson for the day doesn't always come out of a lesson plan that's too patly worked out. I had to re-examine my whole conception of what constituted a meaningful teacher-student relationship. My standing up beside a blackboard yakking away at a dutifully attentive and captive group simply didn't get it.

What was a teacher? What was a student? What was teaching? What was learning? If it was true, as I taught, that we are all members of one another, then it followed that we all had things to teach and learn from one another.

A precocious 12-year-old dentist's son with a passionately idealistic plan for getting the U.S. out of Southeast Asia and back on its spiritual feet; a 16-year-old black unwed mother from East Oakland with a flare for writing and a serious drug problem; a young Chicano who felt totally useless until he discovered the worlds of poetry, drawing, guerrilla theater and 8mm filmmaking, thereby opening up possibilities as to how he might personally contribute toward effecting revolutionary change; a 13-year-old girl from Chinatown who takes karate lessons, plays piano, is into needlepoint, types 55 words a minute and writes gentle quiet poems about her uncles and dreams, and resentful ones about wasteful government and moonshots; a black high-school student from Oakland who comes on hostile at first to everyone around him but who quickly got into things and later writes: "... Birth of the moon/the splitting of an atom/death of the moon//the enlarging of a brain tumor/silky jungle of a spider, a turtle//cloud of darkness hovering above life/symbols of death, destruction, and the user/of evil things/a fish man/a man strapped out in the sun to bake and dry out/an ape man// . . . fish arguing with each other/dirty colors/beware of cigarettes." Two junior highschool girls who hand in journals kept over a 3-week period for me to read that are so intimate and crackling with detail from their pubescent Now world (filled with drugs, innocent sex and loaded guns) that make me determined to get to know and understand them better. These are a handful of the young people whose lives touched my own.

After Patricia Parker, a young black poet well-known around Berkeley and San Francisco, came to read her work to the NYC workshop, one of the young men, Nathan Griffin, author of the above-quoted *Birth of the Moon* poem, came up to me afterwords and said, "You mean that was poetry? What the sister was reading is poetry?" "That's right, That's one kind of poetry." "Well, maaan, I always thought it had to rhyme and stuff and have the same number of words in each line or something. I think I might even try to knock out a couple of em now! I didn't know you could tell it your own way."

These were beautiful moments for me, events that I'll never forget.

Did these workshops ever produce any budding young writers of promising talent? Who knows? Who cares? One or two people may continue to play around with writing. The point is that writing and reading and talking about one another's work was a way of being together, of relating to one another at some very fundamental levels. As far as most of my "students" were concerned, parents and teachers, most older people, in fact, were impossible to get to. They were locked into their own little self-righteous shells. Trying to write and hear the sound of their own voice was a heavy experience for many of these young people. I got to see how something like poetry, when it's for-real and not dealt with or presented as some kind of cabalistic construct impossible to decipher, can really open up a lot of doors and windows. Great literature, so called, frightens youngsters like L.K. Wallace because it's been so stuffily touted and often for the wrong reasons. After finding out how hard it was to write, he fell into reading books, peeking into them to see how other people did it and what they had to say. He didn't want to tackle any book, however, that he didn't think promised to be a pleasurable experience.

"The very substance of literature is experience," writes Aldous Huxley in his 1932 introduction to the Black Sun Press edition of the 16-year-old Raymond Radiguet's novel *Devil in the Flesh*, "and experience is what is most difficult, in the nature of things, for a child to have. It follows, therefore, that even a suitably gifted child will find it very hard to produce good literature. To some extent, it is true, the child of genius ... may know intuitively and by imagination, things which other people can discover only by coming into direct contact with brute facts."

The fact is that I have a need to write about and teach the beauty of certain inner and outer spaces, the miracle of being alive, the necessity of changing the way we live with one another and with the rest of nature. I can't do this without being able to learn continously from those who are newer to the world than I am. The teaching of writing has been one of the ways in which I've been able to keep in touch with the young.

Mildred Nobleton, age 15 at the time, a former NYC workshop participant, writes it up this way:

WRITING (*word, language, or what?*)

> Come!
> Where?
> It's safe here.
> But not anymore.

Someone has taken this
   quiet place
and disaster has struck.

Come out of your shell!

EASIER SAID THAN DONE

The Essex, 1963

What 21-year old Billie Hill actually sang on that record was: *My buddies tell me/fly to him/sigh to him/tell him I would die for him.* But for reasons now perfectly understandable, I picked up the line as: *My bodies tell me/fly to her/sigh to her . . .* and on and on under Paris skies.

Paris had done that to me; turned me around and slipped me into one of those high-flying moments that floated like a red-white-and-blue balloon of being high above the Eiffel Tower on up into autumn clouds that crowned the City of Light.

Don't ask me why I had to go all the way to France to tune into The Essex, an American combo—and a Marine Corps musical unit at that! But there I was, and there it was: the naive, sincere rock-and-rollish sound of them, bouncing from a jukebox in a Left Bank *brasserie*. The music wasn't anything special, yet it was indeed what American poet Colleen McElroy, an Army brat who grew up on bases in Germany and elsewhere, would later refer to as *Music From Home* in her sweet, sweaty book of the same name. I had been absent from the United States just long enough to crave the watered-down musical equivalent of turnip greens and blackeyed peas and cornbread that this unexpected *hors d'oeuvre* symbolized.

I'd been absolutely in my element—or so I thought—hanging around outside the Blue Note, too out of pockets to get in and give jazz saxophonist Johnny Griffin a proper hearing; quizzing a lightskinned, expatriate hawker of the international edition of the New York *Herald Tribune* for subway connections; remembering Django Reinhardt and the Quintet of the Hot Club of France; wandering the Champs Elysées and drifting around Montparnasse; pondering the great American writer Richard Wright's prolonged residence in what I regarded as the hometown of the bourgeoisie; and soaking up the icy after-effects of colonialism through chance encounters with Senegalese, Algerians and other lowly paid people of color.

Ah, but there was a woman, a heady young woman, dark and quietly voluptuous. She could've passed easily as a native of that northwestern region of Spain known as Galicia. Afternoon and night we would rendezvous and parlez-vous in each other's sparkling hotel rooms. Living, by the way, at the same hotel helped.

My bodies told me fly to her, sigh to her, sing for her, swing for her, and it was all so deliciously mutual. Everytime I found myself knocking at her door or opening mine to her gentle tap, the whole of Paris would light up at once to soothe the ache and joy of human love with "Easier Said Than Done" as our theme song.

COME ON-A MY HOUSE

Rosemary Clooney, 1952

At 13, I'd listen to anything. Well, almost. I wasn't crazy about Lawrence Welk or Guy Lombardo, but the gates of my mind were still swinging wide open most of the time, and when I read somewhere about how much Louis Armstrong loved the sound of the Lombardo band before it migrated south from Canada, I was ready to open my ears and give even the Royal Canadians the benefit of a doubt. Besides, there was no particular sound back then that was supposed to be hipper than any other. The concept of hip might've penetrated the strictly jazz world, but it hadn't made much headway yet in the middlebrow midwest where everything was still in flux.

My favorite disk jockey from that matchless pre-smoking era was a fellow named Bob Murphy who billed himself as the "Tall Boy, Third Row" and broadcasted weekdays over WJBK in Detroit. Murphy's idea of putting a show together was to line up a stack of records that suited his fancy, no matter what the genre, and to take it from there. His theme song, of all things, was Boyd Raeburn's "Dalvatore Sally." Now, it must be remembered that, of all the far-out big bands of the day, Raeburn's was probably the one that stood the least chance of ever being rounded up and brought back into the fold of convention. His band was to Stan Kenton's what I suspect Fletcher Henderson's had been to the Duke Ellington orchestra—an inspiration. It wasn't unusual to snap on my little metal encased Arvin bedside AM radio and hear Murphy open a show with Sonny Rollins performing "The Stopper," then jump to the Four Aces and Johnnie Ray or those harmless Chordettes of Arthur Godfrey's Talent Scouts fame. Then the Tall Boy Third Row might turn around and drop a Nat King Cole trio side on you, or a Charlie Parker—or, right smack dab in the middle of that groove, he might crank up Rosmary Clooney's "Come On-A My House," her early Fifties runaway hit staged by Columbia arrangement and repertoire man Mitch Miller, and composed by a couple of amateur songwriters named Ross Bagdasarian and William Saroyan.

William Saroyan. That's the name that set off a buzzer in my busy head. I couldn't believe he'd been in on the making of this jumping pop number laced with quasi-immigrant Eyetalian lyrics (or were they supposed to be Armenian?) that spoke of "figs and grapes/and a pomegranate, too." There was a jazzy harpsichord churning up sand and grit with the rhythm section accompanying Rosie, as she's called by showbiz intimates, and that too—given the Saroyan connection—sounded entirely appropriate and very much in the spirit of everything I'd read by then of this eccentric California writer whose homemade prose style was profoundly endearing to a gangly, gawking pubescent like me. My very awkwardness seems to have ripened me for the kind of unbridled bravado and enthusiasm for life that Saroyan's short stories and conversational soliloquoys championed.

Routinely, I read everything I could get my hands on by Saroyan, and when the World Stage—a theater-in-the-round company in Detroit's Highland Park—put on his play, "Across the Board on Tomorrow Morning," I was right down front on opening night. And I made it back for a second helping. By then I was in high school and rather inclined to think of myself as a writer. I was publishing in *The Central Student,* our school paper for which I was features editor and a local jazz and cultural tabloid known as *Idioms.* Along the way I'd managed to wangle an actual press card as an occasional columnist for something called the Detroit *Tribune,* a black newspaper with a Christian Science slant whose publisher was a man named Fruehauf of the trucking corporation Fruehaufs. So I figured I wasn't doing badly for a teenager. Like all adolescents with artistic leanings, I took myself seriously, too seriously, and, as Saroyan once said of his youthful self, I was intense. Poetry poured out of me like leaky fountain pen ink, and—to use the parlance of standard, not black English—it was *bad!*

William Saroyan's the one who showed me it wasn't always necessary to go by the rules. That is, it was more than possible to say in writing what you and you alone had to say about your own comings and goings, your own experience in the world, and say it in your own voice, even if that voice quavered at times and what it had to deliver was almost unspeakably dumb and wrong-headed. In short, style, zeal, enthusiasm, sincerity and bravado could carry you a long way when it came to getting your heart and mind down on paper. "In the time of your life," he says in his best known play, "live!" I got the message.

The clock, indeed, is always ticking loss, loss, loss. The idea, as I got it direct from the Daring Young Man on the Flying Trapeze himself, was to relax and have fun while you're out there on the page. As a fledgling scribe with no sense whatever, and as one who was yet to come to terms and make his peace with form and structure, that message was worth at least half the world to me; a hemisphere anyway. It whisked me out of step with many of the knowledgeable and well-schooled writers I came to know once I'd slipped into the University of Michigan at Ann Arbor, but it also kept me going.

Over the years, I continued to fall in and out of love with

William Saroyan's work. His output was tremendous, and only recently did I learn how much the man actually wrote. I heard his daughter Lucy on the radio one morning—a morning not long following his death—telling about how she and her brother Aram, as children, were forbidden to interrupt Daddy at home while he was working. She further mentioned that his published work is only the tip of the iceberg, so to speak, and that the unpublished manuscripts far outnumber all the work that's ever seen the light of print. Gradually, poring over his stories, novels, essays, memoirs and the letters literary scholar and historian James D. Hart has shown me, I've been able to piece together more than I care to know about the man who, because of American tax difficulties, took up residence in Paris in the late 1950s at 74 Rue Taitbout.

For years that address has remained in my Rolodex file under Saroyan's name. Something told me I'd be running into him one day. It was only a matter of time and timing. I thought about him a great deal when I moved from Michigan to the San Francisco Bay Area in the early Sixties, and for a time I was traveling to Fresno to play a coffeehouse gig one weekend a month. The day after President John F. Kennedy was assassinated, my guitar whiz buddy Perry Lederman and I were wheeling into Fresno to knock down fifty bucks apiece as folk and blues performers. It was a Saturday night—November 23, 1963—and I can still reconstruct the unspoken sadness that hovered over the meager crowd we played for. It was even more acute than the malaise we'd felt the night before at the Cabal in Berkeley when nobody on the bill had felt like going on, and least of all myself. Something had ended or was about to end. Every one of us could sense it. The minute we pulled into Fresno, which I'd only known through Saroyan's eyes and ears and childhood grasp of the town's meaning, I turned to Perry at the wheel of that beat-up Studebaker and said, "Saroyan's town."

"What'd you say, man?"

"Said, Saroyan's town, this is William Saroyan's town of grapes and sun and immigrant Armenians."

"I don't see no grapes," said Perry, "but I'll bet they'll have some wine at the club. You really like that guy's stuff, don't you?"

"He's taught me a lot." And at that very moment, unbeknownst to Perry or anyone else in the world of Hello-Out-There, I was quietly transported to a place that didn't so much exist in time as it did in one of those intuitive flashes in which past, present and future fuse. In that instant I took in the winking neon lights of downtown Fresno, focused on the memories locked up inside me of two Armenian women I'd secretly loved in highschool and at college—the one, a zoftig, brownskinned girl whose beauty was only rivaled by the black and Jewish beauties in the immediate community; the other, a sleek, blackhaired, fairskinned honey who used to work the check-out counters in the food lines at East Quad, Ann Arbor, the University of Michigan, back when I'd been a busboy there in 1957.

But also playing around the edges of this stopped and quivering vision of timelessness were all the musty, forever renewable seed impressions of Armenian-American life that William Saroyan's nutritive prose had planted in my fertile mind of long ago. *Life*—that's what those stories and sketches and vignettes and plays had all been about; the untellable history of the human spirit. Of course, of course! Saroyan had *created* all this stuff about his childhood and youth in Fresno and elsewhere. Sure, it was all based on actual events and real people—whatever that meant—and yet the key to understanding that world somehow lay in knowing, nay, *realizing* that Saroyan was at all times only being himself, an artist, a writer with a generous yet fragile point of view or slant on things that was inextricably tied to his own delicate and complicated hunches, insights and beliefs.

It would be years before I found out about the problems he'd had dealing with his own family as father and husband. It would take even longer to learn that the man who wrote so winningly about family love and warmth had never had an easy time of it himself. Certainly those years, those painfully formative years Saroyan spent in an orphanage must have affected him enormously. And the heavy drinking, compulsive gambling, monumental restlessness and globetrotting were doubtless symptomatic of a deeply disturbed personality. That's one way of looking at it.

But Saroyan was also a compulsive writer and a compulsive observer of life and the human condition whose works are still read and loved all over the world. Often his views were refreshingly naive, even dead wrong, and he wasn't beyond waxing sentimental or maudlin at the drop of a hat. He recorded the human comedy as he saw and felt and lived it and—when you come right down to it—the world is far richer than it might have been had he never traveled this way at all. He was willing to take extravagant risks that, more often than not, paid off handsomely. Imagine holing up for a month in a room to write simultaneously a whole novel *(The Adventures of Wesley Jackson)* and, over the same period, keep a diary about that experience *(The Adventures of William Saroyan)*, both of which appear in a distant volume called *The Twin Adventures.* His award-winning play, *The Cave Dwellers,* was composed in eight days in a New York hotel room. The speed with which these projects were executed is no measure, of course, of the works themselves, but the spirit and gusto that prompted them still stuns me. Why not sit down with a songwriter and come up with "Come On-A My House"? It might just turn out to be a hit.

When my son Michael was five, I took him to see a Jackson Pollock retrospective at the San Francisco Museum of Modern Art. For me the exhibit provided an opportunity to take a fresh look at one of the declared masters of that long-lasting vogue known as abstract expressionism. Like bebop, so-called "action painting" was a cultural phenomenon that had thoroughly permeated my adolescence to the point where I'd almost grown up believing this was the only true way to paint, making all other approaches seem misguided or, worse yet, academic. Fashion is like that; licks and modes have a way of shaping whole eras whose participants sincerely believe that the only way to play jazz was like Charlie Parker, the only way to sing a pop ballad was like Frank Sinatra, the only way to write poetry was like T.S. Elliot, and the only way to paint was like Jackson Pollock.

I walked with my son around the museum, gazing in my late thirties at Pollock's frantically executed swirls, dribblings, spatterings and fat brush strokes which, at one time, I'd felt intimately at home with when it came to appreciating visual art as culture. Culture, what was that? After you get past yeast and yogurt, it can get awfully tricky, particularly when the vernacular civilization you move in is profit-motivated.

When fatigue set in, I sat with Michael on a long marble bench and sighed. "Well," I asked him, "what do you think?"

"About what, Daddy?"

"About Jackson Pollock's paintings."

Michael looked around the stately, immaculately organized room and then at the immense canvas that took up the high wall before us. I imagined how Pollock had probably donned a tall ladder, set up canvas and pots of pigments, dipped his brush, swathed it liberally, then slam-banged and splashed and re-splashed his way across the blank wilderness of canvas. What a way to make a statement!

"Well?" I asked my son.

Not having yet learned to fidget at such questions,

Michael looked at me and at the mammoth painting again. "Daddy," he said, "I paint too, you know."

At that, I laughed and hugged him until he squirmed and wiggled loose. He had no idea what his innocent comment had meant. As far as I was concerned, this was art criticism at its finest and most revealing.

On our way out, by the late Sunday afternoon ticket-taking door, who should pop on his way in but William Saroyan himself. He was dressed for the weather in a London Fog raincoat and floppy gray hat with a black umbrella at the ready. It was the lavish mustache that did it, though; the 1890s mustache and the eyes, those eyes, as sad and twinkly as the eyes of a child about to be dragged from the circus grounds at closing time. O he looked to be about as world-weary as they come, this graying man of letters and notions who was wandering, as if by some divinely silent cue, in our direction.

Just as he stepped within comfortable earshot, I said, "You're William Saroyan."

"Yes, yes, that's me all right." His smile was ready, warm, polite and bright. "And who, if I may ask, are you?"

"Al Young, and I'm delighted to finally meet you at last. I've been a fan of yours since I was a kid."

"You're a writer, aren't you?"

"Yes, I am."

"And what do you write?"

"Novels, poetry, all kinds of stuff."

"Is this your son?"

"This is my son Michael."

"What a handsome lad. How old are you, Mike?"

Michael laid his best sociable giggle on the old man and said, "Five. Well, five and a half, really."

Saroyan shook both our hands and said, "You must tell me the names of your books."

"I wish I had copies of some of them on me. It would be a pleasure to inscribe them for you."

"Don't worry about that. I know how it is. Just give me some titles." He tapped at his temple. "I won't forget because I'll make a point of finding and reading those."

"You still living in Paris on Rue Taitbout?"

Saroyan laughed. "You really have been keeping up with me, haven't you? Sure, but I've got it worked out so I spend a few months over there and a few over here. It's more interesting that way, you know?"

"Of course, I understand."

"So give me some titles."

I felt embarrassed but all the same I mentioned *Snakes, Who Is Angelina?* and *Sitting Pretty,* all the novels I had come up with by then.

"Great titles," he said. "And you say you're a poet too?"

"Listen," I said, "I'll send you copies of each of those books."

"No, no," he said, "I'll find them somehow and I'll read them. I'm still a big reader and I won't miss these."

I believed him and I didn't believe him.

Bunched up in my mind, ready to unravel, were all the topics I wanted to rush out and have coffee or beer with him and discuss at reasonable length—playwriting, publishing, San Francisco, Hollywood, the Thirties, the Forties, the Fifties, travel, Fresno, memoirs, spontaneity, Armenian food, music, that picture he'd posed for from the 1950s in front of a piece of sheet music composed by himself and expatriate American writer and songster Paul Bowles, and, quite naturally, whether there was a connection between music and storytelling and record-spinning and, well, how did he and Ross Bagdasarian just happen to come up with "Come On-A My House"? If only I could get him over to my place!

But there was no time left. The museum was about to close and Saroyan looked as if this might very well have been the last scheduled stop in a long day of making his San Francisco rounds.

With Michael tugging at my sleeve and the clock tocking and ticking and signaling as always, I was forced to understand that this was going to be either the nourishing end or the very beginning of a long anticipated moment that, like the rest of life, would forever be receding like bubbles into the roaring, sloshing sea of memory.

We shook hands again before Saroyan disappeared into the crowd with me watching the top of his salt-and-pepper head every inch of his way.

American through and through, all I could think to remember at that moment was how beautifully timed his arrival and departure had been.

STRAIGHT NO CHASER

Thelonious Monk, 1960

Those were nights when the Baroness would pull up in her gleaming, other-worldly Bentley to fetch Thelonious and motor him away between sets at the Jazz Gallery. The scene was simply not to be believed unless you happened to be there to see it for yourself as I was for as many nights as my lean, practically non-existent budget would allow. Somehow I never worried about money. It came my way in dribbles, but mostly it went. It went for foolishness, and foolishness was a staple for me in those summery times when I was so much older than I am now.

Foolishness sustained me. Foolishness was rambling around the whole of Manhattan, mostly on foot, but also on buses and by subway. I went it alone and I ran in crowds, thinking it possible, as a matter of course, to hear all the music there was, see all the films, read all the books, meet all the people and, in my idler moments, write reams and reams of prose and magical poems to celebrate the wonder of it all and, naturally, just to keep my writing chops up. Oh, and there were languages to learn, and girls; long philosophical chitchats into the night, and entire days whiled and glad-dened away in Hoboken and Brooklyn; ferryboat rides to Staten Island, funky weekend parties, airy beach parties on

Long Island, tuning in nightly to radio bard Jean Shepard, wanderings through museums, hanging around the docks and parks, crashing in strange friends' and friendly strangers' rooms and apartments, learning new things on guitar and ways of deepening and stretching the singing voice, sitting at a Village curb with Dennis Rosmini (guitar Dick Rosmini's pint-sized cousin) and sketching on cheap paper with cheap pencils the disappearing world as it zoomed and wobbled before our eyes.

Am I romanticizing? Am I licensing myself to poeticize what, after all, were only quotidian, dissolving events in the formative era of a simple-minded kid whose head and eyes and ears and nervous system all needed shrinking at the time? Perhaps, I am. But that's only because this was the way I lived it when and while it seemed to be happening—these things, these foolish things that continue to remind us of ourselves when we're in the sorcerous process of becoming ourselves.

And Thelonious Monk was as much a part of me then as he is now. All kids who listen to Monk's music seem to love it at once. It's a child-like music; compelling and attractive in a fundamental way. There's no way, really, to put this all in language (spoken luggage), but when has being at a loss for words ever stopped a writer?

On one of those nights, one crazier than usual, I spent a rapt three sets at the Gallery with my guitar buddy Perry Lederman and with Gordon Hope, a drinker with writing ambitions. We had put away a gang of ale and cheese, crackers and onions over at McSorley's Irish Saloon, and now we were checking out Monk who had Coltrane with him just then. It was also a night when Steve Lacy was sitting in with the group on soprano saxophone. Charlie Rouse was the other horn man. Actually, Monk and Trane were being featured separately as a double bill, but Trane's energy level was such at the time that he managed to ease in on Monk's sets with no apparent strain.

The setup was fascinating. Lacy had just recorded his first album on Prestige which included the Monk compositions, "Bye-Ya" and "Trinkle Trinkle." For formal reasons, Monk had Lacy sit all by himself off to one side of the little stage, and when it came his turn to solo, Lacy would stand and play while the rest of the band provided him with serious, intensive backing. It was like a microcosm of the kind of situation you'd expect to run up against in Johannesburg or in Monk's native North Carolina, but not at the Jazz Gallery.

I don't know why that detail of spatial arrangement registered with me so deeply. Black soloists, after all, had long been featured with white bands as island performers, you might say; in fact, it had become something of a tradition. I could tell, though, that Monk appreciated Lacy's playing and ideas. That Steve Lacy had also chosen Monk as an inspirational ace and mentor must have accounted for his presence on the bandstand at all. It never left my mind, however, that bop itself had been pioneered by ingenious musicians, some of whom had as their express purpose the creation of a music white players weren't going to be able to steal. And, for a time anyway, Bird and Diz and Monk and others like them managed to pull the wool over the white boy's ears, and some colored ears too. Fletcher Henderson's arrangements had helped float the Benny Goodman band to glory; Sy Oliver had cut the kindling and stacked the logs for the Tommy Dorsey band's success; Glenn Miller had borrowed his reedy, lead clarinet-above-the-saxophones sound from the lesser known Negro band of Eddie Durham and so it went.

This is how the rest of that night went at the Jazz Gallery with its cozy decor of abstract expressionist paintings: Perry sat there stunned set after set, drifting into the music from a folk music and country blues perspective. Gordon kept disappearing into the john to sneak little nips of gin from a half-pint he'd packed. The minute the last set ended, Monk disappeared. He didn't dance offstage the way he'd later do nightly once he landed a long-running gig at the Five Spot; Perry, who wasn't a smoker yet, rushed outside for air. I had no idea where Gordon had gone, but since he was basketball player height, I figured he wouldn't be that hard to locate. Monk, I imagined, would be outside the club at curbside, climbing into the Bentley with the doting, glamorous Baroness Pannonica Rothschild de Köenigswarter at the wheel. To the press she was the Jazz Baroness, but to the tight côterie of musicians she was Nica. Monk had written his soothing "Pannonica" for her, and she had inspired Horace Silver's sultry "Nica's Tempo" and other jazz compositions. It was in her apartment that Charlie Parker had died.

I rushed out into the leafy, downtown summer night, blinded by its artificial brilliance. That's when I glimpsed the scrawny black man being chased, hounded by a pack of white hoods. I blinked and then saw him drop to the pavement, scroonched up in the fetal postion with nothing on but briefs, occasionally flailing his arms and kicking to ward off blows. He was bleeding and kept groaning.

"This is what he gets," one of the hooligans busy kicking him shouted to the crowd. "This is what he gets for goosin a girl in the park!"

The assailants were scuzzy-looking, sallow and ugly like hooligans everywhere. And, like their movie counterparts, they were playing to the flashing camera minds of the crowd gathered at curbside. "For goosin a girl in the park," they shouted. It was a litany.

They kept saying it, all six or seven of them, as if it justified their every savage move: "For goosin a girl in the park, for goosin a girl in the pahk, fuh goozin a goil in da pahk, f'goozin a guheeeyull innapahk, f'goozinagoilinna-pahk, f'goozinagoilinnapahk!!!"

What goil? What pahk? What offense justified any of this? Right away—the music forgotten, the notion of getting another look at Monk and Nica dissolved, the whereabouts of my pals shattered into glassy bits and pieces of meaning like the night with its thousand eyes—I wanted to pull a gun, anybody's from anywhere, and blast them all away, slowly, each by each, as the flames of my anger inched toward insanity—Choom-Choom-Choom-Ka-pyowww! Thunk! Fight fire with fire!

In instant replay slow motion, unknown back then, I can almost chart this pitiful event frame by frame. Suddenly there Gordon stood, cursing and on the verge of exploding, right there on the curb. In real time it was all coming at me so fast I didn't know where start finished or where ended began. Hatred heated the moment. A big old American car was waiting with the engine running and a nervous driver, ready to make the getaway. At first I stood transfixed, trying to size up the scheme. What had really happened. Who was the girl? Who was the young man being stomped before my eyes. Had it all begun in Washington Square Park? When? How? What were we looking at? "Quit it, stop!" I screamed.

Without thinking, I pushed my way through the crowd toward the victim. I didn't know what I could do, but I knew I had to make my way to the front line and let whatever was going to happen happen. The minute I reached the curb, the thugs turned tail and raced into the street to squeeze inside the getaway car, one of them yelling out one last "That's-what-he-gets-f'goozinagoilinnapahk!"

I turned to see Gordon moving toward me from out of the crowd. He looked practically sober with concern and fright. "Al," he said, "thank God, you're OK. I thought it was you they were kicking the shit out of!"

The two of us automatically got to work at once and, with Gordon taking the man's arms and me lugging him by the feet, we lifted the bruised, bleeding man from the gutter and stretched him out on the sidewalk. Someone must have already phoned the police because in no time we heard a siren and could see the twirling colored lights approaching the nightclub. That's when Charlie Rouse, a mainstay with

Monk's band, walked out of the Jazz Gallery, his saxophone case in hand. He strolled to the curb and looked down at the victim impassively.

"What happened?" some latecomer asked from the crowd.

Rouse shook his head slowly from side to side and said, "Humph! I reckon the cat musta fell down. Yeah, he musta fell down."

Gordon got down on his knees and put his ear to the man's face and heart. "He's still breathing," he announced. "But they sure did do a number on him, poor guy."

Perry popped up then from out of nowhere. He said, "If I had me a gun I'da shot the muthafukkas. This is Mafia shit, that's all it is, but I'da shot 'em!"

The cops arrived and dispersed the crowd and cleared the way for an ambulance to park. We were all told to stand back and to go home, the authorities were going to take care of it.

The three of us took the subway to our respective digs, and we spent a lot of time talking about the crazy, disgusting wrongness of it all.

"I'm gonna get me a gun," Perry kept saying. "Can't believe I grew up around here and still don't have a gun. You gotta protect yourself against shit like this!"

Gordon sipped from his bottle and said, "Yeah, that's some terrible stuff. I'm just glad it wasn't one of us."

I don't remember what I said, but I do remember how passive and resigned the crowd had been, and I couldn't get it out of my mind that this had taken place in New York City in the liberal, permissive ghetto of Greenwich Village; not in Alabama, Mississippi or the Georgia backwoods.

"Who were those guys doing the kicking?" I asked Perry.

"Local Italians," said Perry. "They never have liked all these outsiders coming into the Village, and Negroes in particular. I'm telling you, man, you better pack yourself some heat!"

What a way to end a night of beautiful, exciting music!

The subway sped up uptown to our separate but equal

worlds, each of us locked into the pain and anger of that night.

Later I heard that there were repercussions; that a black gang known as the Chaplains—the very ones reputed to have once challenged the New York Police Department to a rumble in Central Park—poured into the Village in taxi cabs and got out dressed in suits and ties, toting neat little business-like attaché cases. Inside those valises were bicycle chains, knives, pipe wrenches and other urban artillery. The way I heard it was that the Chaplains—whom many whites called the Mau Mau Chaplains—proceeded to avenge the brutal beating that'd taken place outside the nightclub by slashing out at any white man who even *looked* street tough.

Although I come from a family of pistol-packing Southerners, right on down to my elderly grandmother and aunts, I never felt comfortable with guns. But Perry did, indeed, get himself a gun, and that's another story. They actually sent the Baroness up the river on a narcotics possession rap. Steve Lacy, like dozens of American jazz artists, moved to Europe. John Coltrane and his music flourished, even to the point of inspiring one devoted cult to build a church around it. Monk quit playing in the 1970s; simply stopped with no explanation and died in 1982. A year later, Gordon died of chronic alcoholism. Charlie Rouse seems to still be on his feet, alive and well and working, with no sign yet of falling down.

And, as you can see, I lived long enough to get this down onto paper, knowing well that—like notations on musical score paper—it'll go on being strictly dead stuff, an artifact, until another human being runs it through that most marvelous of instruments, imagination, and transforms the look of it into sound by breathing sense and meaning and feeling back into these blues.

MY BOYFRIEND'S BACK
The Shangri-Las, 1963

One delicious afternoon in the middle of my 23rd year, I'm stomping out of Tad's Steak House in midtown Manhattan, not bothering nobody, pricking my gums with a mint-tipped toothpick, when suddenly—point-blank—it slaps me upside the head like a number 10 paintbrush saturated with hi-gloss nail polish!

Are they Polish? Are they Bohunks? Are they the ghosts of all those glandular girls who used to bunch together in the hall outside the school cafeteria to nasalize "Crazy Little Mama" by the Penguins? No, these tootsies are rolling in pure, sticky, pubescent syrup—American through and through—and what they're doing to me *live* right there on the sidewalks caked with transistorized sound is shrieking at you rhythmically in tones so primal and insouciant it's all I can do to hold back and keep from bursting out in gritty falsetto yelps to keep up.

Hey, la!/hey, LA!/Muh boyfriend's back!

What's that they're saying?

Hey, la/Hey, la/Muh boyfriend's back!

Are they actually singing about that region of the vertebrate body located nearest the spine; in man consisting of the rear area from the neck to the pelvis?

No, not at all.

Finally you catch on, the way you always have to catch on or forever remain silent once you've been flung against your will into the bowels of some dumb song and have to hear it out before you can work your way full circle back up for air. No, what these vibrant fillies are champing at the bit about is revenge. Yes, revenge, my man! It's as simple as that, and almost as simpleminded.

Of all the ninny songs mindlessly inhaled during my ultra-cool and prolonged I-know-what's-happening phase, this one comes lunging at my adenoids and gonads the way those old doo-wop ditties used to do back when rhythm & blues was news.

The Shangri-La's, I figured the minute I heard them, were the white girls' answer to the Shirelles; that is, somebody else's answer to record producer Phil Spector's relentless string of money-making smash records fueled by girl groups. Years later, when the sidewalks I haunted had shifted to another coast, an unsentimental California scribe- a man sympathetic to classic jazz—would lean across a sunny luncheon table and tell me: "Queen of the slut groups, that's what they were!"

I couldn't agree.

It's all lopsided and odd here in America; the ways we wiggle and wobble from era to era. "Give us your hungry and your poor," we cry, then turn around and do a Dr. Jekyll for a decade in the Robber Baron mode. Maybe that's the way it is with these youthful, schizoid, upstart nations. And maybe it's the same with the nubile and restless daughters of blue-collar aristocrats who don't know anorexia from the corner Rexall Drugstore. All they know is they're hungry for a hit.

The Shangri-La's (as in *La la la la la la la la lahhh-ahhh-la, I love you!*)—like all the others—were only giving the people what they figured we'd like and—so help me Mitch Miller!—they were right on the money.

JUMPIN' WITH SYMPHONY SID

George Shearing Quintet, 1952.

Everybody was bopping by then, bopping and being, but mostly bebopping around Detroit where there seemed to be no end to the expanse of glittery thrills, and you talk about goofiness! That was the order of the day.

Fantasy ran wholesale in the barbecued overtones of those scrumptious chords laid out like some interlocking ladder of sound to the sky, orange-colored like steel mill light leaking up from midwestern valleys to the nighttime hills, to say nothing of the heat, cooled down, cooled out, as cooling to touch as the hot ice they used to store in the garage across the alleyway where all the ice cream sandwich and creamsicle people made their vendor connection afternoons in summer. That stuff would freeze you and burn up your flesh at the same tempo. You raced around trying to erase painful moments by melting and freezing them into the same instant—and, of course, you were what?—12, 13, 14 years old? It was iridescence you were after and that's just what you got, in memory at least. Spatial soulfulness and all that kinda stuff hadn't been installed in the language yet, not in the Midwest yet, not in any way that counted anyway. And what counted? Movement: macking, leaping, jumping (with Sid or without him if your weren't in New York) and allowing all that smoothed-over koko-bop to mess you around in ways it was going to take years to undo.

But then, you never were one to be undone—just reassembled, gently, electrically, with everything intact; only changed like the taste of old well-bottled Seagrams 7 Crown.

You were really hearing Shearing.

CAST YOUR FATE TO THE WINDS

Vince Guaraldi, composer (or, FANTASY RECORDS AS OF 1975)

If a national archives is ever set up for the purpose of preserving significant, whimsical Americana, then room will surely have to be made for some of those memorable records produced in the 1950s and 60s which bear the Fantasy label.

Tucked away in collections all over the world, there must be thousands of those peculiar-looking discs fashioned from brightly colored vinyl—some red, some blue, even a green one here and there. You could see clear through them, grooves and all, which didn't always make it easy to set a stylus down right away on a given LP track.

This imaginary archives would have to be housed in quarters at least the size of Grand Central Station to accommodate even a token selection of artifacts attributable to *homo americanus*—Mister B. shirts, sack dresses, Nehru jackets, Hadacol, hula hoops, pee wee golf clubs, wax false teeth, 500-page novelty catalogs, paper polaroid specs for watching 3-D movies, kinescopes of TV's *$64,000 Question*, calorie counter wheels, B.B. guns, 98-cent Jesuses with suction cups, Edsels, Studebakers, hair relaxers, illustrated dance step patterns to The Turkey Trot, The Hucklebuck, and The Funky Robot.

103

Yes, there would have to be a permanent display devoted to Fantasy Records' early releases; products of a recording company whose history, like that of the music industry and America itself, is uncommonly diverting.

Take for openers, the fact that so many of those old 78s, 45s and LPs were pressed on tinted vinyl. Well, it just so happened that Max and Sol Weiss, Fantasy's founders, were into plastics, not music. Sol, the elder brother, had been experimenting with plastics long before the advent of Pearl Harbor, trying, like countless others, to develop an unbreakable phonograph record.

By 1949, both Weisses were still struggling along in the field of plastic custom moldings. To make ends meet, they were renting the loft space in their building to a company manufacturing a fire-fighting foam known as Firewater. They were also distributing a line of toilet brushes on the side. As if that weren't diversification enough, the Weisses had also started Circle Record Company, a small pressing plant at 654 Natoma Street in San Francisco. Operating in its heyday on a round-the-clock schedule, Circle pressed up Chinese, Hawaiian, hillbilly, classical and Dixieland items for independent labels such as trombonist Jack Sheedy's locally-based Koronet Records which issued the very first singles by an Oakland cocktail lounge pianist named David W. Brubeck.

After Koronet folded and orders for Brubeck's records continued to pour in, primarily from Portland and Seattle, the Weiss brothers decided to take the operation over. Sol, who allegedly had been dead set against the idea from its inception, wanted to call the new lable Reluctant Records. Instead they ended up christening it Fantasy after a popular science fiction magazine. Fans of the genre, they later launched a subsidiary label and named it Galaxy after yet another sci-fi publication.

Light years before Clifford Irving and his Howard Hughes "biography" made headlines, the Weisses had mastered the art of the put-on soundly enough to put it to effective use in the realm of public relations. Employing an approach that might be termed poormouth or po'mouth chic, they let it get around and into the papers that Fantasy was a venture predestined to fail and that they were out to lose as much money as possible in the hope of garnering a whopping tax loss.

When the Weisses signed Dave Brubeck and the pianoless Gerry Mulligan Quartet which featured trumpeter Chet Baker, word went out that they were doing so because they personally thought that the music these men made was simply "terrible" and totally lacking in commercial appeal. Modern jazz, they let on, had run its course. This was in the early 1950s. Brubeck's records began to catch on in places remote from the Pacific Northwest. The Mulligan group, which Max and Sol first caught at San Francisco's now defunct Blackhawk, produced the biggest jazz single of the Eisenhower Era—"My Funny Valentine." Promptly putting its worst foot forward again, as Fantasy legend would have it, the Weiss brothers signed Cal Tjader to contract, the Brubeck drummer who'd taken to playing vibes. Tjader's attractive Latin jazz sound became a staple and has sold steadily and respectably across the years with no sign whatsoever of letting up.

Still determined to fail and come out behind, according to their tongue-in-cheek publicity stance, the Weiss brothers rushed to sign such unlikely candidates for fame as folk-singer Odetta, bluesmen Sonny Terry and Brownie McGhee, poets Kenneth Rexroth, Lawrence Ferlinghetti and Allen Ginsberg, and an arcane, way off-beat nightclub comedian named Lenny Bruce. When pianist Vince Guaraldi recorded the album *Jazz Impressions of Black Orpheus,* intended to "cover" the musical soundtrack of a then popular French-produced movie set in Rio de Janeiro, he just happened to include, to round out the session, an original, gospel-tinged composition on the LP's B side called "Cast Your Fate to the

Winds." The tune, Fantasy's first hit in the early 1960s was, of course, a runaway bestseller.

For the record, though, it must be noted that Fantasy, during its fledgling years, turned down the likes of Jimmie Rodgers, the Limeliters, and the Kingston Trio. When singer Johnny Mathis auditioned, he got shot down too with a breezy, remembered aside from Max Weiss: "Nanny goat music wasn't selling."

Carrying the PR joke even further, Max wrote to *Down Beat* in 1956 and said, more or less, that "the true story of Fantasy Records can best be expressed as a series of failures ... Not major or catastrophic ones, but just that things never go right, and we all sort of find ourselves heading down strange paths. It's frustrating but, by now, we have resigned our company to being the plaything of fickle fate ... a story of emotional, physical and artistic failure, and in only the dollar and cents category has it halfway succeeded. In no way does the fact that it makes a profit detract from the utter failure of its high and mighty aims."

Science fiction aside, the story of Fantasy's ascent from a little label with a whacky image, staked by an initial investment of $1,000, to a formidable multi-million dollar operation is a lot more complicated than anyone's fabled account. Making lemonade from lemons is one thing. Turning vinyl into gold—as any alchemist will attest—is quite another feat, certainly one that isn't performed overnight.

Fantasy/Prestige/Milestone is presently the partnership's official title, and despite its gargantuan triumphs in the pop music jungle, it also just happens to be the largest jazz record company on the face of the earth. Even more remarkable, perhaps, is the fact that Fantasy—the only major record company west of Los Angeles—is still independent.

At least four of Fantasy's chief executives are long-time jazz devotees—Saul Zaentz, chairman of the board; Ralph

Kaffel, label president and former Los Angeles jazz record distributor; jazz A & R director Orrin Keepnews who, with Bill Grauer, founded Riverside Records over 20 years ago and his own Milestone label in the early 60s, each of which blazed beautiful and timeless trails by documenting important jazz developments of the not-so-distant past. Keepnews, incidentally, is probably the only person in the industry who's in a position to re-issue albums which he himself originally produced. Vice-president Ralph Gleason's vast knowledge and love of jazz and its history is pre-eminent.

Gleason (R.J.G. reads the plaque on his office door), veteran commentator on America's music and culture, seems to have been predestined to become a Fantasy executive. As an internationally established critic and celebrated San Francisco columnist, he early recognized the label's peculiar significance and has chronicled its evolution—put-ons and all—right from the beginning. The V.P. title is formal. Gleason is in reality something of a minister without portfolio. He variously sniffs out fresh talent, supervises Fantasy's line of artist promotion films which are offered for exhibit on a rent-free basis, and, along with Keepnews and Kaffel, decides which LPs are going to be released or re-released. By his own admission, he enjoys being on the other side of the desk.

Let's jump back to Saul Zaentz, to 1955, the year that he resigned from his sales position with a northern California record distributor to join Fantasy. The company was already clicking by then with the Weiss brothers at the helm. By mid-1967, Zaentz, who had always wanted to form a record company of his own, was able to buy Fantasy outright from Max and Sol Weiss. "The story's a bit complicated," Al Bendich, former ACLU attorney and U.C. Berkeley professor assured me, "but perhaps I can simplify it for you." Bendich, who once represented Lenny Bruce, among other showbiz notables, presently heads Fantasy's legal staff. He, too, is a jazz, folk music and blues aficionado.

What Al Bendich explained, essentially, was how Saul Zaentz—in the wake of an arduous court battle involving the Weisses, an Audio Fidelity executive named Herman Gimbel and Zaentz himself—assembled the group of investors, 14 in all, who ponied up the $325,000 it took to close the deal.

Shortly before the company changed hands, Max and Sol Weiss had signed a rock group fresh out of Berkeley High who called themselves the Blue Velvets. Remember that tune? Remember that rendition of it that teenage junior flips were imitating all over the country in the early 1960s, *American-Graffiti*-style? Well, not much was happening, so the Weisses changed the name of the group at one point to the Golliwogs. Try calling someone that in England! The guys in the band didn't know about the change until the record came out. They were outraged. They were so pushed out of shape, in fact, that for a good while they simply didn't do much of anything musically.

After Max and Sol sold out, having parlayed their original investment into well over a quarter of a million dollars, the first thing Zaentz did was to re-sign the band which had hit upon a very lucky name for itself—Creedence Clearwater Revival. In almost no time, Creedence broke big and kept right on keeping on, breaking pop charts all over the world with such sparkling, heavy, home-made material as "Proud Mary," "Born on the Bayou," "Susie Q.," "Lookin' Out My Backdoor," "Lodi," "Green River" and "Down on the Corner."

"It was simply incredible," says Bendich. "We were able to move out of this cooped-up office in Oakland into a brand new Berkeley building where our staff rose from a dozen employees to well over sixty."

Creedence Clearwater Revival—whose lead singer John Fogerty was once a Fantasy mail room staffer—managed within the space of a very few years to generate unheard-of profits for this once "struggling" company.

There aren't many, if any, major independent record

producers who can even come close to matching the present-day facilities of Fantasy/Prestige/Milestone. Housed in an attractively designed two-story structure at Tenth and Parker Streets in lower Berkeley, Fantasy is easily distinguishable from most of the industry surrounding its three-acre city block site. For one thing, the building all but glistens in its newness.

Inside you'll find three complete recording studios—one of which accommodates up to 80 musicians—with accompanying control rooms equipped with all the latest attendant hardware and software for 24-track, 16-track and 8-track recording. Mastering and editing equipment is completely up to date with eight natural echo chamber units and, as of this year, an expansive studio for film screenings and the dubbing of soundtracks.

You'll also find, right there on the premises, a charmingly landscaped reception area, complete with tree and other plants. An oldtime penny arcade-style booth occupies one corner of the spacious lobby, decked out with a sign that reads: *RECORD YOURSELF 50 CENTS.*

There's a business office center, conference room, mailing room, and warehouse space. Since all of the LP jackets and promotional graphics are also created and designed here under the supervision of art director Phil Carroll, there's a complete art and photographic studio and a processing laboratory as well. Executive offices, dressing rooms, showers, and even a sauna bath round out the 32,000 square feet of imaginatively utilized space.

Fantasy's director of publicity is an attractive, cheerful-eyed blonde named Gretchen Horton, a journalist who once worked for *Rolling Stone*. While her nine-year-old daughter Pia is sprawled on the office carpet, piecing a rather large puzzle together, Gretchen—between phonecalls and other interruptions, all of them perfectly normal—recounts Fantasy's history for me, explaining how it has come to be known as Fantasy/Prestige/Milestone.

"After we acquired marketing and distribution rights to Prestige, Riverside, Milestone and a few other even smaller labels, we really began to expand, especially in the area of jazz. Prestige, as you know, was originally run by Bob Weinstock out of New York. From the late forties right on through to the sixties he built up a tremendous backlist. Miles Davis, Thelonious Monk, Sonny Rollins, John Coltrane, Mose Allison, Stan Getz, the Modern Jazz Quartet— just a staggering number of jazz greats. We bought the rights to the Riverside and Prestige catalogs and, at the same time, because Orrin (Keepnews) was available and because he had been an instigator and producer of all that we'd bought, we just hired him, too. He came in plain and, after about six months, was made a vice president. McCoy Tyner, Charlie Byrd, Joe Henderson, Bill Evans, Gary Bartz, Cannonball Adderley—these are some the artists he'd worked with in the past. Here, just take a look at our catalog."

The F/P/M catalog, with its hundreds of listings, is impressive by anyone's standards. It reads like a *Who's Who In Jazz and Blues*. A few of the artists you'll find indexed therein are Fletcher Henderson, Earl "Fatha" Hines, Ida Cox, Benny Goodman, Lightnin Hopkins, John Lee Hooker, Jesse Fuller, Mary Lou Williams, Don Byas, Charlie Parker, Dizzy Gillespie, Annie Ross, Yusef Lateef, Mongo Santamaria, Bola Sete, Charles Mingus, Kenny Burrell, Merl Saunders, Archie Shepp, Gene Ammons, the Art Ensemble of Chicago, Woody Herman, and on and on and then some.

The company's eclectic policies in matters of recording enable it to cover many musical bases. Milestone, for example, recently re-issued six marvelous double-LP packages known as "twofers" (a Fantasy concept, by the way, which has set an industry trend) of vintage blues and jazz performances by Blind Lemon Jefferson, the young Louis Armstrong with King Oliver, Jelly Roll Morton, the New Orleans Rhythm Kings, Bix Beiderbecke and Ma Rainey, the classic blues singer who discovered Bessie Smith. Each of these historic re-releases, all handsomely designed and modestly priced, comes with extensive, well-written liner notes that are of invaluable use to both beginning and seasoned collectors of American music.

Around the same time, more or less, that this set of re-issues appeared, several F/P/M artists hit the pop, soul and jazz charts with big-selling albums that are still going strong—McCoy Tyner's *Echos of a Friend*, Flora Purim's *Stories to Tell*, Gene Ammons' *Greatest Hits*, Stanley Turrentine's *Pieces of Dreams* and, most spectacularly, the Blackbyrds' LP *Flying Start* which contains the hit single "Walking in Rhythm."

"The Blackbyrds are our hottest group right now," Gretchen Horton informs me in a soft voice while a track from pianist Hampton Hawes' new album plays pleasantly in the background over the office stereo system. "All five of them are still enrolled as fulltime undergraduate students at Howard University. How they manage to keep up their music and grades, too, well, it's anyone's guess."

It was trumpeter Donald Byrd who launched the group and who has continued to coach its exciting career, having first recorded with them on his own best-selling album *Black Byrd*. Until a year ago, he was Dr. Byrd, a full professor of music at Howard in Washington, D.C. where the study of jazz (or Afro-American classical music) was once heavily discouraged.

The working atmosphere at Fantasy is surprisingly re-laxed. You might even say "laid back." Unless there happens to be a recording session in progress, about the only indication you'll get that commerce is taking place will be by stepping into the busy shipping room or the central business offices. Otherwise—aside from the sound of the record player in the receptionist lobby which highlights the company product exclusively and unobtrusively, almost subliminally—it's a low-keyed and moderately quiet world.

In Studio B, of a mid-morning Friday, a very thoughtful-looking Orrin Keepnews is chatting agreeably with bassist Ron Carter about the upcoming sessions with McCoy Tyner, the former Coltrane pianist. Seated in his leather cap and coat without his instrument, you'd never suspect to look at him that Carter has been for some time now one of the finest and most inventive musicians in the business.

A walk down a corridor whose walls are lined with album covers brings you to the art studio where Phil Carroll is busy putting finishing touches on the jacket of the new Stanley Turrentine LP to be released this spring.

During a brief visit to the newly enlarged dining facility, a young woman staffer talks about how saxophonist Cannonball Adderley, who records for Fantasy as well as produces other artists for the label, sometimes brings his personal chef along to recording sessions. While Cannonball's busy cooking in the studio, his chef's at work in the company kitchen, getting up tasty dishes for the band's meal breaks. Unlike most recording companies, Fantasy doesn't charge musicians for studio or rehearsal time so that they wind up in debt to the label before the product has even been released.

Back in Gretchen's office, the conversation shifts from the music business to cinema. *One Flew Over the Cuckoo's Nest*, a film based on Ken Kesey's novel, is being shot on location at the Oregon State Mental Hospital. Directed by Milos Foreman, the movie stars Jack Nicholson and is being produced by Fantasy's Saul Zaentz and actor Michael Douglas. "Actual patients are playing some of the minor roles," says Gretchen, "but it's those professional actors who tripped me out. I don't know how casting managed it but every last one of them looks absolutely insane!"

Ralph Gleason descends from his second-floor digs to join us. A soft-spoken man who always manages to look and dress as though he were on his way to campus to deliver a lecture on, say, Icelandic Literature at the Crossroads, he speaks nostalgically of *Payday*, the feature-length he produced several seasons back. It's about a country/western rock superstar played by Rip Torn. Filmed partially in Selma, Alabama, *Payday* was Fantasy's first venture into commercial filmmaking. It has already been scheduled for future re-release.

As the beloved luncheon hour draws near, we speak again of music and of some of the label's newer finds. Among them are 20-year-old Patrice Rushen, an extremely gifted pianist from Southern California; saxophonists Azar Lawrence and Gary Bartz; singer Betty Everett of "Shoop Shoop Song" fame; drummer/keyboardist Jack DeJohnette; Brazilian trombonist Raul De Sousa whose first album is being produced by Airto, the former Miles Davis drummer who is married to singer Flora Purim. Other groups to watch and listen for are Pleasure, Side Effect, J.D. Blackfoot and another Donald Byrd discovery, the Three Pieces.

Outside in the inner courtyard parking lot, a lean young man, fashionably coiffed and attired, is making his way toward the lobby entrance, lugging a guitar and a boxed stack of reel-to-reel tapes.

"Are you with Fantasy?" I ask on impulse.

"Afraid not, brother, not yet anyway. But I sure do hope to be one of these days. I'm just dropping off these tapes of our band for them to check out. Got my fingers crossed they'll like 'em enough to give us an audition. All we need's a break, you know? *You* don't work here, do you?"

"Sorry, I don't, but good luck."

"Hey, thanks. I could sure relate to a little change of luck."

Headed down Ashby Avenue onto the Bay Bridge, I snap on the car FM and there's Hampton Hawes again, this time on KJAZ, with bassist Carol Kaye and drummer Spider Webb, playing an invention from *Northern Windows*, his last Prestige LP. I reflect on his life and suffering as related in *Raise Up Off Me*, the poignant autobiography that

Hawes co-authored with San Francisco novelist and pianist Don Asher.

It's bright skies—clear and blue—all the way across the shimmering Bay. Cool sunlight is resting on the radio receiver that enables me to tune this particular music in from all of those other waves of sound out there splashing in the afternoon air. "Bach" is the title of the tune being aired. The sound of it, like that of the ocean, is stimulating and comforting. It seems to be playing my feelings and thoughts back to me, for the moment anyway, in some deliciously precise language.

The sudden thought, as I head into 101's afternoon traffic jam, that music has to be marketed—the same as books, painting, dance, autos, radios and other tangible products of spirit and mind—makes me feel thankful for Fantasy's commendable taste, and pleased about its unique and continuing success.

SOMEBODY DONE HOODOO'D THE HOODOO MAN

Junior Wells, 1967

I grew up in homes where the verbal jam session was a floating and usually festive fixture. Clusters of people were forever talking with one another, telling stories, sharing experiences, observations, jokes, riddles, conundrums, and swapping lies. Our talk was musical. The old folks often quoted scripture and we all mimicked the voices and gestures of others, marbling the fat of our utterance with lean strips of proverbial wisdom: "A dog that'll *carry* a bone will *bring* you one." Much later I would become aware of the Kenyan proverb that goes: "Talking with one another is loving one another." For then it was enough to take delight in the pictures and emotions that flooded my imagination as I went about learning, by ear and by heart, the nature of the world that lay beyond my childhood walls and fields.

I used to curl up on floor pallets in a corner or in warmly quilted beds with the door ajar and, while pretending to be asleep, listen to the grown folks carry on into the night by kerosene lamplight—with crickets or rain or wind in the background—way back up in rural Pachuta, Mississippi and other distant settings.

Language and its stitched-together patterns of sound and beat and melody and pitch was real for me. Those crazy-quilt patches of bright and somber and giddy sound formed the literal fabric of my tender world. They were to be taken every bit as seriously as the very tree stump by the side of the dust road winding into town; that stately chinaberry stump where Uncle John, my maternal grandfather's brother, boasted that he'd once seen a hair-raising haint trot past one autumn long ago, hundreds of midnights before I was born. "He was ridin on a moon-white steed," said Uncle John, "and he was as close to me as you sittin from me now. Old Jack seen it too, like to sked him half to death. Rared back, commence to buckin and jeckin so bad I got gooseflesh!"

But I knew Old Jack. He was still alive and he was Uncle John's favorite riding mule. And I knew what Papa, my grandfather, meant when he'd haul off and say in the dead of winter, "I'm tireda hurryin down there to see bout John's mules. Only thing John's mules sufferin from is the miss-meal colic."

It was all as clear and mysteriously evident as lightning bugs pinpointing the summer-starved nights, winking out their starry morsels of code. My cousin Jesse and the other kids even held long discussions about this. That was probably the way fireflies talked with one another. We figured there had to be some luminous cipher involved that was none of people's business. All the same, we spent hours trying to break the lightning bug code; that is, when we weren't dashing around trapping them in Mason jars to make our own special flashlights. The rise and fall of locust choirs on sizzling afternoons was equally magnetizing. Locusts, in fact, provided the background music for a signal incident that buzzes through my memory circuits to this day.

I'd just finished feeding the chickens and was resting on the edge of the back porch, lazily scrawling letters in the yard dirt with a prized stick, when an old, raggedy, smiling hobo appeared out of nowhere. He wore a faded, floppy straw hat and was carrying a burlap croaker sack. I stood, startled, and looked at once to see what Claude was going to do. Claude was our sleek, black farm dog whose jet keen nose usually picked up everything. But Claude didn't stir; he didn't let out so much as a low growl. That tattered stranger, armed with nothing but a grin, crouched at the porch steps where Claude had been dozing and, nodding a friendly "Hi do?" in my direction, patted the dog on his tick-tortured head just as gently as anyone in the family might have done.

Mama, my grandmother, was coming from her garden with an apronful of fresh-cut okra, snapbeans and green tomatoes. I could see she was as puzzled as I was. Nevertheless, she put on a smile, walked around to where we were and she and the hobo exchanged pleasantries. He wasn't asking for a handout or odd jobs to do; he was only passing through and had somehow lost his way. Mama, her gold tooth fittings flashing in the late sunlight, patiently re-routed him, invited him to pluck a few figs and gather some pecans, then sent him on his way. He seemed harmless enough. But when he was gone, she studied Claude and looked at me, then stepped into the shadows of the porch. Narrowing her lucent brown eyes, she said, "I do believe that old rascal musta hoodoo'd that dog." She said this low under her breath, just loud enough for me to hear.

"Hoodoo!" I said. I must've been seven, maybe eight, and I'd heard the term but never from her lips until now. Its meaning had long been hidden from me. "What's hoodoo, Mama?"

"Hoodoo?" she repeated with a slow smirk that wasn't easy to read. "Aw, that's a kinda magic, whatchacall conjure. You burn candles, you mix these powders, get a holt to a locka somebody's hair or a piece of they clothes, say these words over and over. It's magic, but it's the Devil's magic. See, God got his magic and the Devil got his. Myself, I don't like to be foolin with them hoodoo people, never did."

"Well, how come you say that man done hoodoo'd Claude?"

"Cause that dog ain't got no business layin up and lettin that Negro pet him like that. Didn't bark, didn't even budge hardly."

"But how could the man put a hoodoo on him if he hadn't even seen Claude before?"

"That's what we don't know. He coulda slipped round here one night while we was sleep and sprinkled around some goofer dust. Mighta even had some in his hand or up his sleeve just now for all we know."

"But, Mama, wouldn't we'da heard him sneakin round the house here at night?"

"Don't know that either. Them kinda folks know all this lowdown stuff; that's all they study. The man coulda run up on Claude back there in the woods someplace and hoodoo'd him then."

"But why would he wanna hoodoo Claude in the first place?"

Mama trained her gaze on the chickens and the chicken coop and said, "Can't answer that neither, but I can tell you one thing. If I hear any kinda devilment goin on in the night, yall'll hear me shootin my pistol."

This was the same woman who moaned and hummed and sang spirituals all day long while she worked, and who taught me table blessings and the beautiful Twenty-Third Psalm.

It was in such settings that poetry began for me. Perhaps it is children who understand poetry best. I know for certain that, unlike most people, I never outgrew the need or magic or the curative powers of language. The quiescent greenness of those pastures in which I pictured myself lying down is more vivid than ever, and I can see the shapes of cloud and sky reflected in those still waters. I do not take John lightly when he declares, "In the beginning was the Word, and the Word was with God, and the Word was God." Even now in the Nuclear Era when we're constantly only a micro-chip blip away from graceless extinction; even at a time when the functions of poetry have been denigrated and trivialized, when post-literate societies largely regard poetic expression as a mere amusement at best, I've come to view Creation itself as the actualized speech of the Divine; the unnameable, dream-like essence of some marvelous cosmic presence. Sustained and intensive personal experience and involvement with language has opened both my ears and eyes to the magnitude of the Word and its power to transmute perception and consciousness: reality, if you will.

Such lofty realizations have never been uncommon among traditional pre-literate peoples, nor among the so-called civilized. Hindu, Taoist, Christian, Buddhist and Islamic cosmologies abound with them. Leslie Silko opens *Ceremony*, her fecund novel about Indian life on a New Mexico reservation, with a poem that begins: "Ts'its'tsi'nako, Thought-Woman is sitting in her room/and whatever she thinks about/appears." And in his moving book, *Eskimo Realities*, the humanist anthropologist and filmmaker Edmund Carpenter notes: "In Eskimo the word 'to make poetry' is the word 'to breathe'; both are derivatives of *anerca*—the soul, that which is eternal, the breath of life. A poem is words infused with breath of spirit. 'Let me breathe of it,' says the poet-maker and then begins: 'I have put my poem in order on the threshhold of my tongue.' "

It took me quite some time to learn how poetry has always functioned and flourished among all peoples in all times and places, customarily as a natural component of song, dance, work, play, prophecy, healing, exorcism, ceremony, ritual or communal worship. It was the printing press, among other innovations—to say nothing of altered notions about the place of the individual in the scheme of things—that helped change the way we think about poetry and the Word.

Long before the printed word and stuffy ideas about literature turned up in my life, and certainly long before I became the willing ward of schoolteachers, I was sleeping with words. I fondled and sniffed and placed my ear to their secret meanings. I soaked up the silences between syllables, tested them, tasted the saltiness or sweetness of them, and stared off into their bottomless eyes and down their dark, rosy throats. In a world innocent of ABC's, I dreamed in word-pictures and word-objects and word-feelings. And, like most children who live poetry all day long, I disappeared in between the spaces words made. It is this early enchantment with electrifying speech that abides with me still, inspite of the literature industry, inspite of poet-careerists and their ambitions, and quite inspite of the poetry scene itself.

"I always knew you were gonna be strange," Mama reminded me recently. She's closing in on a hundred now; a tough and beautiful little country woman whose light-drenched eyes can still see clean through me. My father's long gone from this world, and my mother just slipped away too. I've wandered and rambled from Mississippi to Michigan to California; all over this country, all over the world. And Mama's still here, telling me things I need to hear. "Always knew you were gonna be strange. From the time you could babble, you had your own way of talkin and understandin. We would put you on the floor with a funnybook or a magazine while you was still a baby, and you'd start turnin pages and feelin on em, and drift right off into some other world. Never would cry hardly. Long as you had them books to look at, you was happy. I never seen anything like it."

All my life I've been trying to hold onto and expand the joyous purity of those early moments and the magical talk that nourished it. Word by word, line by line, season upon season, poetry keeps teaching me that the only time there is is now.

MY FUNNY VALENTINE

Richard Rodgers &
Lorenz Hart, composers

Not long after she'd roused him in the dark to tell him her water had broken, he caught up with himself in the waiting room on the hospital maternity ward. One other father-to-be lay napping in work clothes on a nearby sofa.

He was trying hard to focus on the Sunday morning football game, but his attention kept shifting from the warm colors of the screen to the black-and-white bleakness outside where rain and mist was washing out another kind of picture. It wasn't always easy to tell which world was real and which was imaginary. The love of such mysteries had made a writer of him.

Birth, death; arrivals, departures; yesterday, tomorrow; dreaming and wakefulness—where did any of it end or begin?

"Well, any score yet?"

The disheveled napper was sitting up and yawning at him now.

"Zip."

"Good." The man squinted at his watch. "I been here all night waiting for this game to start."

"Is this your first time, too?"

"Nah, the fourth time around for me. My old lady's gonna get her tubes tied."

When the nurse appeared to lead him into the delivery room, he felt shaky and vaguely jubilant. The middle of November, he thought. The heart of the rainy season. What a time for a kid to be coming into the world! What if something goes wrong? One of his sister's children, his nephew, had been born retarded. A bit of oxygen at the right time might have worked wonders. Was there ever a right time, though, to die or get born?

Seeing her convulsed in pain with her long legs up in stirrups made his stomach quiver. Her tears weren't at all like the ones she'd shed the time he'd proposed to her at the train station in Madrid. Thoughts of time and distances began to overwhelm him again when he thought about the places where they'd started out and stopped—Mississippi, Massachusetts, Michigan, New York, California, Mexico, Morocco, Italy, Portugal, Spain, France, and now California again. What distance did a soul travel from eternity to paternity and maternity?

He became so caught up in coaching her to work and relax, push breathe, just as he'd been trained to do in Lamaze class, that he had to remind himself to relax. Contractions were coming rapidly now.

"I—I can't do it anymore," she cried.

"Sure, you can, angel. You're doing just fine."

But he was no longer seeing his wife Arl; he was looking at woman in a wholly new light, and the beauty and miracle of her was blinding him with a radiance that outshone the antiseptic brilliance of that hospital chamber.

Meanings of labor, meanings of love—and the meaning perhaps of labor of love—exploded upon him the way entire lifetimes are said to unfold before the secret eyes of the drowning. And wasn't it one of life's oldest secrets or mysteries that he imagined he was glimpsing? What had once been invisible was blossoming in the seeable world, but what was the hidden force that gave it life? Where did it come from, where did it go?

"C'mon," he said, "I can see the head poking out! The hair's all black and wet-looking!"

Her tearful flash of a smile made him think of sunlight; sunlight reminded him of rain, the day: November 14.

The nurse and obstetrician egged him on. "We're practically there," they announced. "One more big push."

"Sweetheart, you've done it! Now, give it all you've got. Atta girl!"

"It's a boy!" yelled the doctor as he pulled the glistening infant from its dark and nurturing shelter.

All pure cliché, the writer in him was thinking by then. But the man was helplessly observing how flimsy words were when it came back down to ultimate truths. One of his own mother's favorite sayings took on a powerful, fresh, deep meaning: "Everybody is somebody's child."

The whole world, in fact, felt like an after-thought. The snipping of the umbilicus flushed him with images of navels, oranges, vegetable and fruit flesh, sailing, boats, salt, the incubating sea; the oceans of eternal bliss that mystics say are real. Just as he'd always intuited, the so-called real and the imaginary eventually connect, for when the doctor slapped him gently on his tiny behind, the baby opened his eyes, saw at once what he was up against and began to bawl.

It was only after he'd kissed her and left the hospital, when he was back on the freeway, driving into serious needle-slanted rain, that he remembered how perfectly timed their son's arrival had been after all. He switched the windshield wipers to high gear, snapped off the radio and thought about the distant day in February, nine months ago to the night, when it had all begun.

DUKE ELLINGTON'S SOUND OF LOVE

Charles Mingus, 1974

Well, Charles, you sat down at the piano and penned this one after Edward Kennedy Ellington died, and now I'm finally getting around to commemorating you in another language; one that's neither so direct nor as magical as music, but readily understood all the same.

Late this afternoon after exercising vigorously on my little circular trampoline—a splendid way for music nuts to work out in rhythm—I slipped the stereo needle into the opening grooves of "Duke Ellington's Sound of Love," clamped on the headphones, stretched out flat on my back on the livingroom floor and practiced breathing to you on your beloved bass, George Adam's tenor sax, Jack Walrath's trumpet, the wizardous Don Pullen at piano, and, behind the drums, behind those drums, who else but Dannie Richmond?

The sounds floated into my ears and down into my throat and nasal passages, and when I inhaled and exhaled its colors—rose, geranium, blue-green, soft brown, yellow, orange, ivory, electric blue and indigo. When my breath stopped somewhere in space and relaxation set in, I remembered "The Chill of Death." It still startles me to think that you composed that piece out here in California at the age of eighteen after learning enough yoga to be able to hold your breath to the point where you thought death could be summoned at will. Whatever it was you saw or sensed while you were drifting out there bodyless must have helped send you into an unearthly spin or scramble that never ended.

Stretched out there on the floor, listening to you, Duke, and Billy Strayhorn blending and merging like that, I caught snatches of the pristine Mingus, the one who used to call himself Baron Mingus back in the 1940s while I was still catching up with Cab Calloway and Jimmy Lunceford and Nellie Lutcher and the Modernaires and Johnny Mercer and Hoagy Carmichael and Louis Jordan's Tympani Five and the Ravens and the Duke himself doing "Things Ain't What They Used to Be" on my father's well-oiled phonograph. Circles of sound, circles of fading away and coming back— all of it pure vibration; the writing of sound upon waves of air, sometimes scratchless but mostly scratchy like the sound of leafy branches brushing against the bedroom window at night. Often I'd find myself oozing into the edge of sleep groove by groove. While I was going through that, you were grown out there in palmy Los Angeles, making records with Lucky Thompson, Marshall Royal, Willie Smith, Lee Young, Miles Davis, Buddy Collette, Britt Woodman, Boots Mussulli, Richard Wyands, Claude Trenier and all those ghostly players who never made enormous names for themselves.

It's funny how things happen the way they're probably supposed to happen. Or is that too just a matter of how you look at it? Like you, I'm convinced now that awareness is the answer, the key anyway, to understanding just about everything. At heart, at its deepest, awareness is what brings us around full circle once we set out to discover life's most important questions, like, what and why and where and who we really are. It's memory that seems to carry us where we need to go looking for answers, and music can awaken and help sharpen our memories to the point where we're forced to understand what sages mean when they talk about the end being implicit in any beginning and beginnings ripe with endings. Am I making sense? Years and years of you in my ear have helped me recall so much about what I used to call "myself." Whose self? You caught my attention when you'd kick back and talk about the many selves you had at your disposal. "You've probably always written the same way for a million years," you once said in a letter. I've never forgotten that, just as I've never forgotten the first time we met. Even though your sound seems to have always been there at the back of my head, buzzing along the arteries of my auditory nerves, there actually was an in-the-flesh first meeting.

It was summer, it was night and I'd been wandering around the West Village alone, looking for the Showcase, the club I'd heard about run by a pair of brothers devoted wholeheartedly to your music. By the time I got there, sweating and excited, it was mid-evening and you were out there on the club steps in baggy pants and polo shirt, quieting grabbing a bit of what passed for fresh air in New York. Awed and skinny, I somehow mustered the nerve to mount the steps and introduce myself, blurting out more than I needed to about how much I loved your music, racing all the way back to "Mingus Fingus," your featured arrangement and solo with the Lionel Hampton band, the Red Norvo Trio sides recorded on Discovery, the 78s you'd put out on Debut, your own label, the *Pithecanthropus Erectus* album on Atlantic, and on and on. You must've figured me for a simpleton—and rightfully—but you were kind and warm and led me up the steps into the Showcase to be your guest for the rest of that night.

And what a night it turned out to be! You seated me right down front, told the management to give me anything I wanted—and all I wanted in 1960 was beer, beer, gallons of the stuff. You introduced me to the band, the current crop of Jazz Workshoppers. There was a piano on the stand, but nobody touched it but you when you wanted to demonstrate something to the rest of the guys.

Between sets you sat at my table and started telling me about a young woman, someone who'd come in a couple of weeks ago to catch the band. One thing led to another and, again between sets, you had occasion to shake hands with her. "And, Al," you said, "do you know what happened?"

"What happened?" I asked, still wrestling with whether to call you Charles or Charlie or Mingus or Mr. Mingus.

You grabbed my hand, placed it on the table, pulled your hand back then slowly moved it close to mine. "What happened," you said, "was sparks flew. That's right, sparks flew when I reached to take her hand. Man, that ain't happened to me since the fourth grade!"

Right about then, who should pop up to join us at the table but the vibraphonist Teddy Charles. You introduced him to me as Teddy Cohen, saying, "He goes by the name of Charles but I call him by his real name, Teddy Cohen. Either way he's one of the best vibes players in the business. Excellent. Teddy's movin, though, movin on up." And then you told Teddy about the woman who had stepped in and made sparks fly. That connection was still very much on your mind. She was a Vassar student; rich and thin— Vassarlean. And because your *Mingus Ah Um* album, just out on Columbia, had been enjoying impressive success for a jazz item; the one with saxophonist John Handy and pianist Horace Parlan and trombonist Jimmy Knepper on "Fables of Faubus," "Better Git It in Your Soul" and "Goodbye, Porkpie Hat" (your tender tribute to Lester Young), you figured it was only a matter of weeks before you might be able to support this sweet young thing in the manner in which she was accustomed.

Ah, males! Ah, chauvinism! Ah, jazz and ah, showbiz! Ah, Mingus, Ah Um and ah, tensions and declensions; the Latinate beginnings and endings of ethnicized Western Civilization! She never did show up again, but when another beauty did who reminded you of her, who had the same coloring and girlish appeal, you put her through a blistering, bebop courtship and married her in a matter of days.

But this was yet to happen, the marriage to Judy, the two kids you'd have by her and all that. For then, for that night, you kept your eye on me and played your heart out with the musicians on the stand: saxophonists Booker Ervin and Eric Dolphy, trumpeter Ted Curson and that drumming dandy Dannie Richmond. When the band struck up "What Love?" and "All the Things You Could Be by Now if Sigmund Freud's Wife Was Your Mother," I knew you'd never gotten over Cole Porter's "What Is This Thing Called Love?" or Jerome Kern's and Oscar Hammerstein's "All the Things You Are." The knowledgeable jazz cutie in me automatically superimposed Tadd Dameron's "Hot House" over the Cole Porter evergreen which was something of a bop flag-waver fanned by the Charlie Parker/Dizzy Gillespie version of it. As for "All the Things You Are," I knew you were crazy enough about it to be capable of stretching that lovely song as far as it would go, chordally and rhythmically, and letting it snap back into place again, still spinning on its string in mid-performance like a Jacob's Ladder yo-yo, going: "Here we go loop-de-loop!"

Charles, the way you wash and roar through me! I still haven't digested what you meant that night at The Show Place when you leaned across the table and said, "I been workin on a book, a long, long book about my life. And since you're better educated than I am, I betcha you could help me with it. You could help me write it right."

"When can I see some of it?"

"Anytime, anytime you got the time. How bout tomorrow."

"Tomorrow?"

"Sure, I'll give you my number and you ring me up and tell me when you wanna come over and we can get goin."

"I'd be thrilled, Mr. Mingus, thrilled!"

128

"Good. It's a big job, but I think I got somethin."

It never happened.

That next day and all the days and nights I tried to get to see that manuscript of yours, you either blocked the way or froze on me. You just didn't want me to see it—not just yet anyway.

Later that year, I dropped in to catch you at The Minor Key on Dexter Avenue in Detroit. By then, except for Dannie Richmond, the band had a whole new line-up and was featuring my old pals from highschool days: Charles McPherson on alto saxophone and Lonnie Hillyer, trumpet. It was the night Dannie didn't turn up for the opening set, and the band blazed on without him. He turned up, though, when you were leaving the stand. He staggered in the front door just as you were setting your bass aside. In front of the packed audience, you yelled out: "Well, if it isn't Dannie Richmond himself! World's greatest drummer. But just cause you great, that don't mean you can come fallin in here anytime you feel like it. Not on my gig, no! Now, I want you to get back there and wash up right now cause you're on!" Then, turning to the crowd, you announced: "And now, ladies and gentlemen, we're going to feature our drummer, *Mister* Dannie Richmond—all by himself!"

And, you know what? Dannie came back out, mounted the stand, propped himself behind his drum kit and took care of business with fire and precision for close to half an hour.

On my way out, I saw you standing by the door in your heavy black overcoat and Russian fur hat, ready for the snow, and I said: "How's the book coming?"

"Great," you said, "it's great." And with a tap at your head you added: "I'm writin one of the best chapters right now, up here."

By February I was on the West Coast, and when you hit town I was right down front at the Jazz Workshop in San Francisco. I no longer thought it necessary to bring up the book. I figured you must've had your reasons for counting me out. Instead I sat the whole night with my arm around a new girlfriend and soaked in all the beautiful sound the way one of those Japanese novelty plants soaks in water and blossoms right before your eyes. In this case, the blossoming was done within my ears.

Those ears have led me in your direction again and again. I don't think I missed an appearance of yours in San Francisco from then on, but it was the summer of 1963 that I got it in my head to make one last attempt at finding out what was happening with you and that book of yours. One starry night, driving back into Manhattan from a party on Long Island with Charles Jr., your painter son, I decided it would be nice to crash where he was staying, which just happened to be at your Third Avenue loft.

It was close to four in the morning when we arrived. I'd no sooner begun walking around, checking out all the stacks of paper and music and posters and albums and books and instruments than the telephone rang. Charles Jr. answered. It was you on the line, and I could tell by the way he was talking that you weren't particularly tickled to find out somebody else was up there, sharing your soul-space with him.

When Charles Jr. hung up, he turned to me and said: "Dad doesn't want you to stick around."

"Hunh?"

"When I told him Al Young was up here with me, he said to keep you away from all his papers and stuff and to get you outta here as fast as I can."

Charles, I was hurt. Well, actually, I was hurt and a little flattered at the same time. I didn't leave before noting that the telephone your son had spoken into wasn't the same as the pay phone you'd had installed on one wall, presumably for the use of visitors, and probably musician visitors at that.

All those contradictions and ironies and reversals and mysteries—they make me feel I'd never truly known you at all. And yet you were always kind and encouraging to me.

You took an interest in my writing, urged me to stick with it, gave me loving messages in person and by postcard, and even turned up one night at a poetry reading I gave years later at the YMHA in New York. You sat there, pretending to be asleep, with Susan Graham, the lovely woman you would eventually marry—the one who was to stick by you after you contracted Lou Gehrig's Disease (amyotrophic lateral sclerosis)—and afterwards you explained how you couldn't linger because you were on your way to a Stevie Wonder concert but what you'd just heard was, in your words, beautiful, just beautiful.

It was Susan, Sue Mingus, who stuck with you to the sad end, who accompanied you to Mexico where, having given up on orthodox doctors, you sought treatments by curanderos and other kinds of healers and medical practitioners. It was also Susan who flew to India, as you had asked, to scatter your ashes over the River Ganges. You were, after all as it turns out, a Hindu by religion.

Between our first mental, physical and final encounters, there's so much that took place that it's impossible to touch upon it all in this sudden communication. Somehow I'll squeeze what little I know of your amazing existence and how it touched my own life into a longer book of some kind; the one I'm writing with Janet Coleman. It'll be a two-sided memoir and she's already finished her half. Charles, why didn't you tell me you'd also made the same offer to her of working with you on *Beneath the Underdog,* that autobiography of yours? And what's become of the thousands of pages that got edited out of the published version?

There are so many sides to you and your music. Playing through it all is the sound of love. *The sound of love, the sound of love*—the words kept flowing with my breath. For years the very thought of love and how music conveys the essence of love has kept me moving in its direction. Your old L.A. buddy Eden Ahbez wasn't talking about human love when he penned the words to "Nature Boy," was he? I can still hear the strings dying down behind Nat King Cole as he beguiles and reminds us: *"The greatest thing/you'll ever learn/is how to love/and be loved/in return."*

Were you the one who put Miles up to recording "Nature Boy" for your Debut label? I can hear love in the way he plays it, just as I can hear the love you felt for Ellington in your music; the Ellington of "Mood Indigo" and "Sophisticated Lady" (You called yours "Invisible Lady" and "Bemoanable Lady."), and the Ellington so intimately associated with Billy Strayhorn that many people still think Duke wrote that astonishing "Lush Life." Flowing through all of this sound is some manner of love that can only be described as divine and immutable; a love so complete and overpowering that when we are real, when we abandon our temporary selves—as sometimes happens under the influence of music—we find ourselves partaking of a joyfulness that seems endless, that lies achingly beyond the things of this world. And why shouldn't it be so? Music, after all, is vibration, and we are vibration. Soul is vibration and so are thoughts and feelings and moods. Piquancy and frequency can make sparks fly, especially when it's a matter of the tune and the attuned becoming one. Tuned to its grandest level, music, like light, reminds us that everything that matters, even in this world, is reducible to spirit.

Charles, I know you know what I'm talking about. I miss you and the little talks we used to have when you were still around, the world wound around your massive frame like weighty chains of events. Eventually, though, like all musicians for whom practice of this God-given art is nothing less than religion, you must've heard the sound of that love, somewhere down the line, and it must've turned you around and around. Your worldy alternative just happened to be food—like, the days when you'd walk around with a greasy brown paperbag leadened with those porkchops you plucked and nibbled like potato chips—but for others it was strong drink (spirits), or heroin, cocaine, unbridled sex or the stunning rush of money and fame. But you knew these were only tacky, tenth-rate approximations of the real thing.

All the Mingus stories continue to pile up: Your gargantuan appetites, the time you punched out So-and-So, the night you cussed the audience out, and on and on. *Beneath the Underdog* even helped contribute to some of this apocrypha, this scuttlebutt. All I do now, though, is listen to the legacy you left. That way I can keep the record straight. Listening and hearing you speak in your original language, music, I have no trouble whatever following the sensitive adolescent who wanted to play cello in a classical orchestra, but who, being black, had to learn instead to slap that bass!

You always had a reputation, Charlie, for being good with your dukes. I love the way you handle this tribute to Ellington. And while you're at rest, I simply want you to know you're still loved, now more than ever—but that's life in the bebop business. I still love you madly, wherever you are.

BUT BEAUTIFUL

Kenny Dorham, 1957

Originally it was Kinny, not Kenny, because the name his parents gave him when he was born in Texas in August of 1924 was McKinley Dorham. He started out playing tenor saxophone in the 1930s and ended up a trumpeter, or, rather, a remarkably well-rounded musician who played, composed, arranged, and also sang.

Musician lore can be as endlessly diverting as it can be pointless. Everyone has his or her favorite stories about this or that musician; their feats, their excesses and, above all, their idiosyncrasies. Like music itself and the pleasure it gives, such anecdotal hearsay can be entertaining and, in some instances, illuminating and privately meaningful.

It's fascinating to know, for example, that the youthful Johann Sebastian Bach, jumped one night by a gang of his own choristers, brandishing sticks, was able to defend himself with a sword so ably that his attackers had to back off and turn tail. Such extra-musical information may or may not affect the way in which you listen to "The Well-Tempered Clavichord." The point is that if you love the music, you will probably be interested in knowing the facts and legends surrounding its creators.

Kenny Dorham—or K.D., as he was called by his friends—

was certainly no legend in his own time. The truth, though, is that he was—along with Roy Eldridge, Dizzy Gillespie, Fats Navarro, Miles Davis and Clifford Brown—one of the very finest trumpet players in modern American music. During his brief lifetime, like countless other artists, Dorham's journey along the road to recognition was largely unpaved. According to those who knew him, he knew who he was and well aware of the extent of his talents.

"Actually, I'm one of the better trumpet players around," trombonist Al (Wardlow) Hassan remembers him as saying. "Listen to me. You can hear it. I can get around on the horn better than most." Hassan, a chum of mine since high school days in Detroit, played in Sun Ra's Arkestra for several years and gigged with Dorham at a Brooklyn club called Turbo Village in the mid-1960s.

"K.D. was so good-natured and personable," Hassan recalls, "that he threw me off-guard at first. Musicians, especially in New York, aren't always as easy to work and socialize with as he was. K.D. was a beautiful horn player, and fun to be around too. There'd be nights when he'd tell me beforehand what he was gonna bring off in his solos, and then he'd get up there and *do* it! I was young and quite impressed and kept wondering why this dude wasn't better known."

Non-musician admirers have expressed similar views of Dorham's abilities and personality. Poet/novelist Ishmael Reed fondly recalls his frequent encounters with K.D. at the Port of Call, a popular West Village cabaret in the early 1960s. "Kenny was a delight to be around," Reed says. "I was always glad to see him. For one thing, he had a fascinating mind and his interests went well beyond the music world. He was a ladies' man, a gentleman and a creative observer of the scene. I always bought him a drink—he liked rum—because I enjoyed his company and knew he was great."

As far back as the 1950s, Orrin Keepnews, the veteran jazz activist and writer who originally produced many of Dorham's most valuable sessions for his and Bill Grauer's historic Riverside label, was singing his praises. "Kenny Dorham," he wrote in 1957, "is by now established as one of today's major trumpet stars. Like all the trumpet men who came up in the bop period or thereafter, he has had to serve several years of what might be called involuntary apprenticeship: overshadowed more than a little by those style-setting youngish 'elder statesmen,' Dizzy Gillespie and Miles Davis. But that apprenticeship can now be considered to have been left far behind him.

"A rich-toned and powerful horn man, whose approach to jazz has always been marked by freshness and buoyancy, 'K.D.' has in recent years also displayed a steadily developing maturity of conception. By now, both his fellow musicians and an ever-growing percentage of the jazz public have recognized that Dorham's trumpet speaks with its own personal voice, that he is an individual valuable artist. In short, Kenny Dorham has arrived."

These remarks turned out to have been overly optimistic: the man was actually never to stop paying dues during his lifetime, but he certainly did begin paying at an early age. After serving in the Army in the early 1940s, Dorham played around the San Francisco Bay Area before trekking east to work in big bands headed by Dizzy Gillespie and Billy Eckstine. It was during this period that he also wrote some impressive arrangements for Cootie Williams and Lucky Millinder. There's a 1946 recording of Thelonious Monk's "Epistrophy" by Kenny Clarke and his Rhythm Boys on which Dorham, barely of legal age, takes a short, halting solo that's probably best described as strained. Even so, you can sense in that embryonic outburst a hint of the kind of urgency that would later mark his mature style.

After the war, Dorham worked and recorded with Mary Lou Williams, Sonny Stitt, Fats Navarro, Lionel Hampton, James Moody and Charlie Parker, among others. Saxophonist John Handy reflects that he "learned a great deal about music from K.D. on those early Dial recordings he made with Bird." During the Fifties, Dorham joined Art Blakey's Jazz Messengers and later, after Clifford Brown's tragic passing at age 25 in 1956, he toured with the Max Roach Quintet. Brown's soulful ballad "Larue," recorded by Dorham that same year, is an affectionate tribute to a profoundly gifted fellow trumpeter. The Sixties saw Dorham leading his own groups extensively, working with such veteran luminaries as Jackie McLean and Hank Mobley.

Drummer Max Roach, in a distant *Down Beat* profile, once confided: "Miles Davis says that the only people he can hear on the horn today are Dizzy and Kenny. And I know what he means. When he wants to hear an inspired horn he listens to them." Roach later told Orrin Keepnews that "Kenny can get some things going that are really *abstract!*"

To many of today's musicians and listeners, the term "abstract," as applied to the arts, might carry more of a pejorative overtone than it did in the Fifties when people— seeking relief from the barrenness of that era's bland mass culture—were turning in considerable numbers to abstract expressionist painting, foreign films, folk art and, as always, to jazz, that good old homemade American music that had become by then an internationally vital musicial idiom.

"Abstract," as Roach intended it, doubtless referred not so much to Dorham's playing being theoretical or abstruse (nowadays we would say "conceptual") as it did to the richness and economy of what he played; his graceful ability to pack so much meaning into his vigorous lines and statements without recourse to clichés.

In fact, one of the most marvelous aspects of Kenny Dorham's horn work—which, by the Fifties, had reached full maturity—is its originality. In his hands the trumpet sings the way it does to the kind of life breathed into it by a Louis Armstrong, a Jabbo Smith, a Henry "Red" Allen, a Bix Beiderbecke, or a Clifford Brown.

Unlike so many bop-nurtured soloists, K.D. rarely fell

back upon stock phrases or mechanical configurations or borrowed licks to sustain or fill out a solo. Always respectful of melody itself, he phrased from the heart. He sang. "About the only thing I ever heard him play that even came close to a cliché," Al Hassan attests, "was the way he had of bending a note. It was his trademark, really. That's how you could always tell it was him. He didn't bend them like other trumpeters. He'd sing the note on his instrument."

He sang with his voice too, as can be heard on a recording he made of "Since I Fell for You," Buddy Johnson's bluesy, ageless ballad; one we little kids, especially the girls, tried to sing like Savannah Churchill on the Mississippi and Michigan grade school playgrounds of my childhood. Of Dorham's vocalizing, which was publicly debuted during his mid-1940s stint with the Gillespie big band, Keepnews had this to say: "While it *is* closely allied to his playing, it is not (as is so often the case) just a sort of vocal imitation of his trumpet style. It is clear that Kenny is quite aware of a distinction, a difference in approach and function between the two. Thus, unlike most musician-vocalists, he does not just stress sound-for-its-own-sake; he has a singer's appreciation of the 'message' of the lyrics."

It's fun to compare his mature trumpet work from one period or setting with that of another. I happen to love the way he backs up Abbey Lincoln on their recording of "Don't Explain," that haunting Billie Holiday gem. In each instance, no matter who he was playing with, Dorham's utterances, marked by subtle timing and phrasing, are as fresh and unassuming as a young, new-blossoming lotus plant responding to sunlight. The more closely you attune yourself to his sound and what it's saying the more you experience emotionally.

The album *But Beautiful* offers a rare opportunity for listeners to hear Kenny Dorham in a fertile variety of settings peopled by such top-flight musicians as Sonny Rollins, Hank Jones, Oscar Pettiford, the legendary Wilbur Ware,

Cannonball Adderley, Paul Chambers, Philly Joe Jones, Jimmy Cobb and Ernie Henry, to name only a few; all too many of whom have already departed this earth. Alto saxophonist Ernie Henry, a man whose crying tone is said to have deeply influenced Eric Dolphy's sound, died in 1958, suddenly, at the age of 31. He can be heard on that LP on what were to be his last recordings.

Dorham endured and, seemingly, made the most of his own brief life. "He loved to play," Al Hassan tells me, "and he loved to live. He was, in a sense, a man of the people. He loved having them around. Even when things got rough and he had to take a job as a salesman in a music store in the 1960s—Manny's in New York—he was still enjoying himself and functioning creatively. He liked to have a good time, and he wanted everybody else to be happy."

After playing more and more infrequently for some time, largely because of a worsening kidney ailment, McKinley Dorham died in December of 1972. He left the world a treasury of beautiful music to enjoy. This story is told that when he showed up for pianist Wynton Kelly's funeral in 1971, many of his fellow musician mourners were disturbed by K.D.'s unkempt appearance, and his embarrassingly ragged overcoat in particular. Dorham couldn't have cared less about such a reaction. He had come to pay his respects to someone whose music and friendship he valued. That was all that mattered.

Music was Kenny Dorham's way of paying his respects to the living and to life itself.

WHAT A LITTLE
MOONLIGHT CAN DO
Billie Holiday, 1935

I can't tell you what my daddy was up to in 1935 when this joyous little ditty first came out, but I know good and well he couldn't have missed it because Ben Webster was on it with Benny Goodman, Roy Eldridge and Teddy Wilson, and Dad was a Webster listener from way back.

I can tell you for a fact, though, when "What a Little Moonlight Can Do" finally hit me smack in the solar plexis. It was on a totally lunar night on another side of the world, down in Western Australia, a little spot in the bush that went by the aboriginal (read: original) name of Wundowie. Sounds like someplace secreted way back up in the piney woods of the Delta, don't it? Wundowie, Mississippi. But never mind, there's a whole new moon that's got me talking in tongues, for the moon can be so milky and moveable on certain warm nights in tropical regions I swear you can almost hear it moo.

Close to half a century after she'd recorded it, Billie Holiday's wonderous "Ooo-ooo-ooo!" caught up with and wafted me away deep into one of those primal nights that's nestled at the heart of all nights. We're talking root nights here; we're talking summertime in Australia—what we'd still regard as winter on this side of the globe—when skies of the Southern Hemisphere are crammed with planets, stars, shooting stars and astonishing constellations. Not only did it take my breath away; the upside-down and all-turned-around view of the heavens available Down Under was enough to melt and freeze my subtlest feelings; fix them in amber and press them under the kind of glass that will always be more spirit than they ever were the connect-the-dots menagerie of pop astronomy I'd been trained to remember.

At one point that night the sky became so alarming and magical in its magnetism that every single one of us gathered there at Brian Dibble's ranch—Sherry Hopkins, Fran Richardson, Altamira, John and Chris Allert, Jan Berry and poets Roger McGough, Rosemary Dobson, Chris Wallace-Crabbe and Phil Collier, among others—cut our loving talk short, set down our beers and got up to check out what was going on up above us. That's when Billie Holiday started playing through my American brain.

It was also the night I'd been traipsing around the surrounding paddocks with my feeble Instamatic camera, hoping for a kangaroo to show its face. Everyone had been making fun of me, the poet as tourist. Jan Berry, a lovely blonde New Zealander immigrant and interior decorator, said: "Al, if no kangaroos turn up for you to photograph, do you think you'll ever come back?"

"Shoobee-right-might," I told her, striving for coolness in my Yankee approximation of the all-purpose Aussie rejoinder: "Should be right, mate!" From what I'd observed during my whirlwind visit, the phrase seemed to cover everything from "How's it going?" or "Do you think it's going to rain?" to "Do you think she'll survive?" and "What say we call it a night?"

That night I wanted to resurrect Billie and give her a big hug for having transformed that otherwise neglible pop tune from the Depression Thirties into something lasting. I still haven't heard anyone else who's been able to bring it to life the way she did. But that's genius for you. Billie could sing the words *lonely* or *flower* or *heaven* or *flame* or *soul* or *happiness* or *sky* or *romance* or *kisses* or *love* or *moon* like no one else. She'd make you taste them on your secret tongue the way she lived and loved in the bittersweet world we share in this dreamy wakefulness where word and touch and glimpse and fragrance and flavor and feeling keep dissolving, melting us into that eventual ocean of bliss we seem to be looking to drown in on the sly.

Billie, if you're out there listening somewhere, I just want you to know about one lovely night in Australia, of all places, when the sound of you at the back of my heart rose to the surface and helped the moonlight do what moonlight does so simply and gloriously.

Talk about your love at first sight, it was a little bit of all right. Ooo-shooo-be-dooo-be—right. Might.

And, as if that weren't amazement enough, some kangaroos actually showed up.

WHEN I LAY MY BURDEN DOWN

(Traditional Negro Spiritual)
Tuck & Patti "Live," 1983

Synchronicity. That's the term coined by psychologist Carl Jung to describe the mysterious process by which seemingly disconnected events fall into place or click. Synchronicity isn't always being in the right place at the right time; it's also being there with the right stuff. It's magical when it happens, and I happen to be a long time believer in such magic, yet, again and again, I'm tickled by it.

Take, for example, the recent Sunday morning when I sat down to a continental breakfast with pen and paper in hand to map out my reflections on guitarist William "Tuck" Andress and singer Patti Cathcart, two exciting performers with a fresh, irresistible sound, currently active on the California scene. No sooner had I sampled my juice than the sweet strains of a familiar melody, a spiritual, floated into the diningroom. I pushed my notes aside and laughed. The young Haitian waitress—this was in Washington, D.C.— had turned the corner radio to a program of local church news and gospel music. My ears were basking in "Glory, Glory"—also known as "Lay My Burden Down"—which also just happens to be one of the fieriest selections in Tuck's and Patti's eclectic, ever-growing repertoire. Pop, jazz, soul, rock, Beatles, standards, rhythm and blues, Brazilian, folk, gospel—this pair does them all justice, joyfully, tastefully, and always with a feeling that makes you glad your ears are attached to a heart with a life-giving beat.

Propelled by Tuck's inventive accompaniment, which can be heated or eloquent by turns, Patti can deliver this inspirational classic—and other material equally beautiful—in tones so warm and healing and infectious that, on occasion, I've felt as though my very body were being suffused with something subtler than sunlight or ultraviolet rays.

The first time I had the pleasure of hearing this gifted duo was on a lazy, windy Sunday afternoon in concert at the New Varsity Theater in Palo Alto. Their magnetism was unmistakable; I was profoundly moved. It was early 1981. I was just back from an energizing journey to Australia. And, as it quietly happened, Tuck and Patti, I would learn later, had barely returned themselves from a six-week pilgrimage to India; specifically to the rural village of Ahmednagar, burial site of the late and saintly Meher Baba, a holy man revered all over the world whose simple teachings continue to inspire these gifted musicians' lives.

"The effect of that pilgrimage on our music," Tuck says with more than a hint of intensity in his normally calm voice, "was dramatic, and not one we'd anticipated. You hear people talk about 'The India Effect'—sort of a glow that people come back with. Our experience was we came back and did a concert at the New Varsity."

"That was amazing!" says Patti, turning her lovely face my way. "That was the first time you'd come to hear us. People were crying; half the audience was in tears. We'd been having very good nights working the room upstairs, but nothing like this."

We didn't even play well that day," Tuck continues, "but nobody knew it. We felt that somehow, for whatever reason, we were working as vehicles. There was so much of an interplay of love."

At this, he and Patti exchange one of those gentle, knowing glances. They're lounging side by side now, totally at ease on the sofa in the afternoon half-light of the modest duplex they rent on a muted, leafy Menlo Park side street. Hanging on the wall above and behind them is a striking oil portrait of a dark, smiling man with congenial long hair and a generous, William Saroyan-style mustache. Suddenly something clicks. I'd recognize that face anywhere. In essence it's the same visage I used to glimpse out of the corner of my eye 15 years ago from a certain on-ramp approach to the Bayshore Freeway. Perched on a shabby house rooftop, this peeling yet picturesque billboard proclaimed: *Don't Worry, Be Happy, Baba Loves You*. "Only in San Francisco," I used to think as I was nosing my car frantically into a lane of oncoming traffic.

Patti, who once directed the Second Baptist Church Singers in San Mateo and sang with a gospel group called Messengers of Faith, explains the portrait: "That was painted by a blind artist from South Carolina named Lyn Opt. Baba let him touch his face for half an hour. The blinder Lyn got, the better he painted. I find myself being attracted to Meher Baba because I'd seen a picture of him that looked exactly like Christ in my childhood mind. Christ is my one and only first love. For me it wasn't going to India to worship Meher Baba; it was the worshipping of God and being around people—in any form—who are expending their lives thinking about God. I know some people have a hard time with that."

Patti reaches for a cigarette. "Music soothes," she says. "It's healing. There's this line in *Chariots of Fire* where the main character says, 'I know God made me for a purpose, but he also made me fast, and when I run I feel his pleasure.' I love that line because I feel that way when I'm singing."

Patti loves movies, too. Once, not long after I'd first heard her sing, she sat rows in front of me at a theater showing *The Postman Rings Twice,* the re-make, with Jack Nicholson and Jessica Lange, of James M. Cain's enduring story of erotic obsession. The film focuses unblinkingly on the violent, sexual aspects of a dark, illicit affair. I couldn't help noticing Patti Cathcart's reactions. She wiggled in her seat. She laughed and cried with all the rapt involvement of a child, wide-eyed and armed to the teeth with popcorn and soda, transfixed by fireworks on a Fourth of July night.

Such unabashed love of life is evident in everything Patti does, and particularly in her singing. When she gets up suddenly and moves to the far end of the sofa where the Ecologizer Air Freshener is plugged in, I watch her finally light that cigarette she's been gesturing with like a eager schoolteacher waving a piece of chalk. Unlike Patti, Tuck is a strict vegetarian, a non-smoker and contemplative in temperment. He doesn't exactly strike me as being thrilled about Patti's smoking, yet he does seem tolerantly undisturbed. All the same, she is careful to do her exhaling directly into the electronic filter as though it were a microphone.

An air of peacefulness hangs over their apartment which is pleasantly cluttered with records, books, fretted instruments, sheet music, score paper and other simple furnishings. It would be easy for a visitor to their home to come away with the impression that Tuck's and Patti's true religion is music.

Tuck Andress's parents had no church affiliations whatever. Completely orphaned in his early teens, Tuck remembers his father affectionately as an oil company executive who was also an amateur jazz pianist. His dad had once led dance bands around Tuck's native Tulsa. It was a highschool chum, however, who turned Tuck on to records by the likes of Miles Davis, early George Benson and the man whom he has come to regard as the consummate jazz guitarist—Wes Montgomery. "To me, Wes was absolutely beautiful on those very late albums which some people dismiss as being commercial. He still could play, even though he did go for the money, and whatever he played I thought was golden, really."

Tuck learned the fundamentals of the instrument working around Tulsa with rock and funk bands, black bands in particular. He played off and on with the then unknown Gap Band for years, and he later studied jazz guitar with Dave Creamer of Alameda whom George Benson has called "the most incredible guitarist in the world." But he also listened hard to what he calls "the great bands and the great soloists," and, using his analytical and intuitive faculties, absorbed what they were doing. "By working very hard to get into the emotional content of the music, which wasn't native to me at all, I could get deeply into jazz and play it with a high degree of authenticity. I just started where I walked in the door. At this point, almost everything musical is history. There's not a real new style coming out in jazz right now. And certainly bebop is history, particularly for people our age. It could've happened in the 1700's. It happens to have happened recently enough that we can have some associations with it. We're not living bebop the way Charlie Parker did. It's been developed as far as it's going to go, pretty much. I'm not talking about lifestyle, but on a musical level." Tuck further maintains that his on-going study of music has formed his taste which is, indeed, eclectic. Like the cryptic and iconoclastic Miles Davis, Tuck feels it isn't necessary to suffer to play the blues. "I'm an example," he states coolly, "of someone who didn't have to suffer very much at all."

To my ear, Tuck's snappy, exuberant guitar sound also owes much to an Oklahoma aural tradition that has also nurished such outstanding players from the Sooner state as the legendary Charlie Christian and the matchless Barney Kessel. Certain environment affects musical expression just as it affects speech, even in the era of condos and shopping malls. Since taking up guitar at age 14, Tuck Andress has either performed or made studio recordings with Chaka

Khan, Leon Russell, The Gap Band and Les McCann, among others. One of those "others" is the tireless and ubiquitous Bob Hope with whom Tuck has toured. In the early Seventies, he enrolled at Stanford to study either math or engineering—he wasn't sure which—and ended up a music major. There he studied classical guitar with Stanley Buetens before dropping out of college.

San Mateo, California-born and bred, Patti Cathcart knew from the age of five that singing was what she was going to do. "My grandfather used to train race horses," she says. "So when the off-season would come, we'd go around to these different farms. I remember being at Hollywood Park a lot when we were little kids. We went to this big farm, and I remember lying in this big field—it was really dramatic, but I was a dramatic kid—and something said to me, 'Sing, it's OK, don't worry, that's what you're gonna do.'" Her parents migrated to California from Texas during the Second World War to work as pipe-fitters in the Bay Area shipyards. There were four kids in all, Patti is a twin. "My mother insisted that we play some musical instrument. I wanted to play flute, but we couldn't afford one. Violin was much cheaper to rent than any of the other instruments. My father had a beautiful voice. He said, 'Sing!'"

Patti got the message but, beginning in the fifth grade, she also studied violin for eleven years. A highschool vocal teacher named Art Lande took her under his wing, and later she would study voice with Owen Fleming, former associate director of the Boston Symphony. While still in her teens, however, Patti worked furtively in little bars and juke joints up and down the Peninsula, occasionally doing sets in the San Francisco after-hours dives. Billed variously, but never seriously, as "The Queen of Soul" or "The Queen of the Blues," she performed the kind of music that pleased crowds in those places. "The audiences," she says with impish jocoseness, "were regular working people. Well, actually, they were drunks and other people up to no good. I'd get up and sing 'Stormy Monday Blues' or 'Summertime' or whatever the local hit happened to be at the time. I really had no idea what I was doing; I was just playing a role. If my mother had walked in, I don't know *what* I would've done!"

By the late Sixties, Patti was adrift in New York where, as she puts it, "I was trying to be the female Jimi Hendrix." She sported a rainbow-colored Afro and outrageous velvet suits. "I didn't grow up in an atmosphere where I had to suffer, but as soon as I left home, I went and threw myself into this situation of being in New York with not a dime, singing with a band called Occam's Razor, living in a place where there were junkies all around—although, luckily, I was never touched by any of that—because I thought that was what you *had* to do. I was brushing my teeth one morning in this little horrible hovel, and suddenly something just snapped and went, 'Wake up! Get yourself a job and get out of here!' "

She cut herself loose from Occam's Razor, landed a tough day job at a cosmetics factory, Revlon, in New Jersey and, at length, made herself over. Upon her return to California, she accepted a slot as featured vocalist with Aaron "T-Bone" Walker, the blues great and guitar wizard who composed the immortal "Stormy Monday Blues." Before long, Patti was performing or recording with rock bands such as Kingfish and Gumbo. "But I knew my rock and roll days were numbered," she says, "because I was thinking stuff that wasn't hitting it, that was beyond rock."

Tuck and Patti communicate and work so well together that it's hard for me to believe that they only met in 1978. Call it synchronicity or chemistry, whatever you like; they seem to have been meant for one another. The vehicle, if you will, who brought them together was poet and saxophonist Mike Stillman, a graduate of Stanford. By chance, Stillman urged each of them, individually, to audition for a Vegas-style show band in San Francisco. The band never got off the ground, but Tuck and Patti clicked almost at once. "I prayed for two days before the audition," says Patti. "Prayed all the way up there. I needed a change. My life was not happening. I said, 'God, I'm dedicating my music, everything that comes out of my mouth from now on, to You.' I rang the doorbell, opened the door and walked in the room, and there was Tuck."

For some time, Tuck and Patti have been a sensation on the California Peninsula, attracting a solid and growing following. It was San Francisco publicist Jan Zones, another music and movie lover, who was responsible for getting them booked into the city's Plush Room in the spring of 1982 and into the Boarding House with Jackie Cain and Roy Krall that summer. Zones also paved their way into the Fairmont's New Orleans Room for their very first, long-term engagement.

As for the future, Tuck and Patti are busy expanding their repertoire and writing some original material to add to the 175 numbers they already know. Mike Stillman, who is also a gifted lyricist, has contributed impressive vocalese versions of many jazz instrumentals to their book. These include winning classics like Clifford Brown's "Joy Spring," Tadd Dameron's "Our Delight" and "Hot House," Charlie Parker's "Barbados," Miles Davis's "Nardis," Lee Morgan's "Sidewinder," and a sprinkling of originals by Chick Corea, Bill Evans, Duke Jordan and Duke Ellington. Because Patti found the words to Billy Strayhorn's "Lush Life" too sad, Stillman sat down and penned new ones. In keeping with their belief that music is an expression of God's love, Tuck and Patti are mindful of the lyric content of the songs they perform.

I find it remarkable—and a little baffling—that artists of Tuck's and Patti's caliber haven't made a record yet, but their plans also call for producing one soon on their own. Neither has ever been in any hurry. If anything, they have quietly resisted the gaudier lures of Show Biz, confident nevertheless that they'll eventually outgrow their peeling identity as "cult performers." In October of 1981, the month that marks both their birthdays, they finally acted on another unrushed decision and went out and got married.

As luck would have it, I caught up with them again in the New Orleans Room one Friday night in 1983 when Joe Pass walked in. Pass, an impeccable jazz guitarist, stood drinkless by the bar to soak up a bit of their set. Patti sang Van Morrison's "Moon Dance," Wendy Waldman's "Mad, Mad Me" and Bob Dorough's "I've Got Just About Everything I Need." Tuck soloed leisurely on Wes Montgomery's bluesy "Up and At It" and on Carlos Santana's flamenco-flavored "Europa." It was thrilling to watch Pass applauding vigorously when Tuck and Patti were finished; clapping and shouting, "Bravo! Bravo!" Dizzy Gillespie and singer/pianist Bernard Ighner—who wrote and recorded the memorable "Everything Must Change"—were also in the room. They, too, were all grins and enthusiasm. At Igner's table during intermission, he told me he was on his way to Italy to record with Sarah Vaughan some of Pope Paul II's poems which have been set to music. This chance remark made me remember that Tuck and Patti will be traveling to Italy in August where they've been invited to perform in concert at the annual Meeting of Friendship Among Peoples in Rimini on the Adriatic seacoast. In the past, guest participants to this festive, week-long event have included His Holiness himself.

I laughed again when I thought about how the clicks were registering that night. The last time my path had crossed with that of Joe Pass was in Perth, Western Australia. He was working with the formidable Oscar Peterson Trio, and we had all gotten together for dinner after a night of unforgettable music. Tuck and Patti, Joe Pass and a music-crazed writer—we all seemed for a moment to have come full circle and clicked.

BOLERO

Maurice Ravel, composer

When Luciana Savignano, a flesh-colored leotard her only attire, went into her dizzying tabletop spin at the close of "Bolero," magnificently spotlighted so that every warm droplet of flying sweat was illuminated in an effervescent spray as it spiraled around her like a wet, protective aura, I practically trembled in my seat, then, glanced over at my friends—guitarist Tuck Andress and singer Patti Cathcart— and saw that they too were astonished!

The crowd of more than 8,000—aroused like the sailor-suited male dancers performing with the lovely Luciana on stage—rose at once to give her and the Corpo di Ballo del Teatro alla Scala di Milano a deafening ovation. We clapped and shouted and stamped our feet and called for, nay *demanded* an encore.

"I really can't believe this!" Patti turned to tell me and Tuck.

"Me neither," I said. "I only hope we draw a house one-fourth this size tomorrow night. Scary, isn't it?"

Tuck, who doesn't talk much, just beamed in the dark and nodded.

The remarkable thing was that we were functioning at all that Sunday night. Our Alitalia flight from Chicago to

Milano had been, for the most part, sleepless. In Milano it was necessary to race by auto from Linate, the international airport, to Malpense Airport for the connecting flight over to Rimini. Signor Marco Grampa and his wife Fabia, who had kindly driven us to Malpense, were amused when I tried out some stuff on them in Italian I was planning to spring at the poetry and jazz concert we would be giving at the 1983 Meeting per l'Amicizia fra i Popoli (Meeting for Friendship Among Peoples). In broken English, he politely corrected my pronunciation in places and then, in a deeply respectful tone, said: "But, Ambassador Young ..." Arl and Michael, my wife and son and I had a laughing fit. They had actually mistaken me for Andrew Young, former U.S. Ambassador to the United Nations, and a guest of the Meeting from the previous year. I explained to Signor and Signora Grampa and their young daughter—in appropriate terms, of course—that if I were in fact Andrew Young, there was no way I'd be fooling around with all this raggedy luggage and no State Department limousine.

But we'd made it to the resort town of Rimini by the Adriatic in sizzling August, exhaused and totally discombabulated. I thought Arl was going to have to be hospitalized at once. Stefania Gioia, our delightful young guide and translator, had been there to meet the plane and to inform Tuck and Patti and me that we didn't have much time. We were going to have to check into the Park Hotel right away, wash up, have dinner, then proceed immediately to the theater where we'd be performing the very next night.

We'd been invited to participate as a featured act in this week-long cultural celebration. In the States we'd call it a festival, but the youthful Catholics who put this remarkable annual event together frowned upon the word festival. None of us had ever seen anything quite like it. From morning till long after midnight, the Meeting offered music, theater, dance, film showings, art displays, panel discussions, lectures, sporting events, a book fair, a technology exhibit—

everything. And it was strictly non-profit; all the organizers, assistants, performers and participants (right on down to drivers like Marco Grampa and translators like Stefania) volunteered their services. My novel *Who Is Angelina!* had just been brought out in Italian by Jaca Book *(Chi È Angelina?)* and the publisher, Signor Sante Bagnoli—at the suggestion of music critic and translator, Luciano Federighi-had arranged for us to take part in this profoundly moving event. You could actually feel the energy, the love that brightened the occasion; the unmistakable spirit of love, for everyone believed in the idealistic purpose of this Meeting.

And so there we stood—Patti, Tuck, myself—amazed that we were still able to keep our eyes open, applauding like crazy for the dancers to return. Even though it was already pushing midnight, time no longer seemed to matter. We had already slipped past the barriers of time and fatigue, and were now clearly operating on the high-voltage energy of the throng. I could feel myself being buoyed and revivified.

At last Luciana Savignano and the men again took their places on stage. The music, once it resumed, was telling; the ballet company hadn't been prepared for such overpowering acclaim. They proceeded to re-enact the subtle, beguiling "Bolero" from scratch, and that was perfectly OK with us and the rest of the crowd. Rapt and inspired, totally turned on, we had the pleasure of going quietly bananas all over again.

It was close to two o'clock when we got back to the hotel that morning.

That Monday night, still vibrating with energy and inspiration from the previous evening, the three of us went out on that same stage. On one side, a gigantic screen had been set up to project photographic slides of U.S. life in color, and on the other side another screen to project translations of some of the poetry and prose selections I'd be reciting. Little skies of butterflies were flitting about our insides at curtain time, but somehow we sailed effortlessly through a three-hour program of music and poetry, with no intermission, that evidently went over big. The show, to use the parlance of *Variety*, was boffo! Tuck brought the house down and had to pause in the middle of his solo performance of Carlos Santana's "Europa" and wait for the unison chanting and clapping of the crowd to subside before he could continue. Patti stopped the show too with her soulful, joyful-blue singing. And the audience even tanding-room-only crowd of more than ten thousand, paid admission. My son Michael, thrilled, excited and perceptive, said, "Daddy, you must've been scared!"

For the rest of the Meeting, we were celebrities, stars: people rushed us for autographs. There were interviews, press conferences, flashbulbs, the works! At one press conference it was my turn to get excited when Luciana Savignano herself turned up. I tried to be cool as I approached her for an autograph, which she shyly profferred. When I asked her how it felt to have to dance "Bolero" twice in one night, she brushed her long, dark hair to one side, laughed and told me in Italian, "Never again! Next time we prepare an encore. I've never ached so much in my life!"

I told her she'd been a inspiration, but I wondered if she truly understood. I also keep wondering what Maurice Ravel could have meant when he said: "I have written only one masterpiece. That is 'Bolero.' Unfortunately, it contains no music."

A lot he knew!

How much does any of us know, coming right down to it, where music and spirit are concerned? Vibration and frequency, call and response, energy, synergy, empathy, sympathy—it's all a mystery, but O so lusciously played out in this overnight dream in which we're all stars, really, shining beyond the tolling bells of sunny Rimini so easily by the sea, by the sea, by the beautiful sea.

THE BIG HURT

Miss Toni Fisher, 1960

Fresh out of Michigan and crossing the Bay Bridge into San Francisco on the lonely F Bus, it seemed I could see the whole color of the world once and for all. I was in my early twenties. It was windy and sunny. Openings to the unverse were loosening up for me, for I was in love with something very special, or perhaps it was with everything at once. From this bend in time, it's hard to say which because poetry kept seeping out of everything I squeezed.

Rooms I inhabited, for example, were sleepyheaded expanses with nothing but oceans shining out of their windows, lighting the sky and all its doubles.

Why it took Miss Toni Fisher and "The Big Hurt" so long to seep up from my subconscious sea and roll over me like a sympathetic wave is also mystifying, particularly when I look back and survey the flood of sweet- and not so sweet-nothings I gave conscious attention. I rather suspected that Sam Cooke's "Chain Gang," Brook Benton and Dinah Washington's "You've Got What It Takes" and The Drifters's "Save the Last Dance for Me" might be around for a few seasons. But what was it about Brian Hyland's "Itsy Bitsy Teeny Weeny Yellow Polka Dot Bikini" or the Hollywood Argyles's "Alley Oop" or the Everly Brothers's "Cathy's

Clown" or Elvis's "It's Now or Never" that could possibly last? I was wrong, of course, just as I was wrong about Marty Robbins's "El Paso," Brook Benton's "Kiddio," "Walk Don't Run" by the Ventures, and Brenda Lee's "Sweet Nothin's."

And who in the world did I think I was anyway? Certainly no Tin Pan Alley shaman or shaper of wham-bam-thank-you-ma'am runaway hits. It was all I could do to pull my own act together enough to hit the road and make the right bus connections.

Dreaming out the bus window midway over the Bay Bridge, swimming in the electrifying violet-blue of twilight, far from the homey simplicity of the flat Midwest, I could feel it begin. Twilight to dawn. California, there I was; right back where I'd started from; alone with myself and face to face with a sea of possibilities.

"The Big Hurt" surfaced like a nourishing lament. It zithered across the evening sky like a shooting star, its smoking tail a trail of quivering sparks.

"The Big Hurt" was pure theater; a dramatized sadness that began in the mind and played to the heart of some odd need to applaud that fragile part of myself that liked to sit in the dark and feel blue.

MOONLIGHT SERENADE

Glenn Miller, 1939

What had brought me back, of all things, to a clear recollection of the dreamy part of my Gulf Coast childhood was the silvery sound of Glenn Miller's "Moonlight Serenade," that slow dance jewel that had hovered around me for over forty years like the aura of memory itself, incandescent and audible and calming like balmy waves washing a shore on a festive night in late summer.

This comforting sound had always resided in a posh dance hall by the sea—all of it imaginary—on certain moonlit nights with all-American couples, elegantly suited and gowned, partying and gabbing and gliding and sliding toward dawn in movies and radio shows and comic books. Images of Archie Andrews and his arch rival Reggie horsing around with Betty, Veronica and Jughead continue to play in the Tuxedo Junction of my mind. Like countless other sub-American kids, hot-house-bred in ghettoes, on farms, near coal mines or across the tracks, I felt cheated and left out of these lunatic good times.

All this sentimental glitter flashed into my head the night I boarded a Houston bus in my early forties. The sign posted above the driver's seat for all to see said: *NO SMOKING, RADIOS SILENT.* But, of course, the driver himself was puffing on a cigarette and had his AM/FM radio going. All the way from Holcomb Road where I got on to Fannin Street where I got off at the Medical Center, we were the only ones on the bus. The driver was roundly tuned to the local nostalgia station airing "Moonlight Serenade." I sat in that seat up front across from the driver and basked in the reediness of the Glenn Miller Orchestra.

"That's some soothing stuff you've got going there," I commented politely.

"Well, yeah," he said. "I try to keep it a little on the listenable side."

He was gray-haired, paunchy and ornery-looking; the kind of guy who might actually draw you into a heated argument about the weather.

I said, " 'Moonlight Serenade' just keeps on coming at you, don't it? All my life it's been like that."

"You know," said the driver, "I believe in giving the passengers a break from this rock and roll. This old boy that works the morning shift, hell, he wears em to a frazzle with that boogie stuff he blasts. The way I figure is people get enough of that junk, so my idea is to calm em down and relax em some."

"This is certainly relaxing," I told him.

"Lemme tell you something," he said, leaning forward as he cut his wheel to make a sweeping lefthand turn onto Fannin Street. "Out here where I live—and I wanna tell you it was white people living nextdoor to me when I first moved in, before I went away and come back then they'd slipped some colored in on me—buddy, lemme tell you . . . they keep that jungle beat goin all day and all night long."

Mind you, the driver, a white man, was telling me this while we were still the only two people aboard, passenger and driver, bumping along in the cool Texas night. Perfectly aware of my color, the shape of my nose and the tight, spiraling texture of my salt-and-pepper hair, he was telling me this.

I let a few more bars of "Moonlight Serenade" slip by before I said, "Blacks aren't the only people who go in for rock and funk these days."

That's when the driver's face lit up and he turned to face me fully as we approached my stop.

"Hell," he said, "I know that! We're gettin to be just as bad!"

ALL THE THINGS YOU ARE

Jerome Kern, composer

Over the years I've stopped keeping track of the worlds crammed inside this blossoming song of praise. But I'll never forget September of 1983 on a slow, thunderous afternoon in the Arizona desert, an afternoon crackling with lightning and bracing winds, when this song broke open like the bud of a Saguaro flower for the wind to catch and dispatch its fuzzy seed messages and send them parachuting in all directions.

After watching blue lightning dance in the distance, against a wallflower backdrop of mountains, Lois Shelton and I motored back from the Desert Museum to her cozy house in Tucson; a house she shared with her husband, the poet Richard Shelton. There in their glassed-in livingroom where I could look out and see that a storm was brewing. I sat to tinker at their grand piano while Lois ducked out to the kitchen to make coffee. A perennial beginner when it comes to piano, I began plunking out notes and mashing out chords to the most hesitant, reluctant and thoroughly rudimentary version of "All The Things You Are" imaginable, with no thought of how it was sounding. When Lois meandered into the room with a gleam in her eyes and her arms outstretched, singing Oscar Hammerstein the 2nd's actual lyrics in bell-like operatic tones, I almost fell off the bench.

She sang: *"You are/the promised kiss of springtime/that makes the lonely winter/seem long,"* and somehow I managed to make the opening changes. By the time we reached the bridge, however, I had grown so intensely involved with rising to her level, which was obviously professional, that to this day I can't tell you whether I was hitting the proper chords or simply inventing them as we went along. My head was saying: F minor 7, B, B-flat minor 7, E, E-flat 7, A-flat major 7, D-flat major 7, G7, C major 7 and all like that, but my fingers were strictly on their own.

When we'd reached the end of it, I sighed, looked up at Lois and said, "Where did you ever learn to sing like that? What a shock! Why didn't you tell me?"

Once she got through quivering with laughter, she flashed me her earthy "Hey, Sailor!" smile and said, "My training was in opera."

I promptly apologized for my lumpish accompaniment but Lois, gracious soul that she is, said, "You were fine, just fine. I couldn't resist coming in on you like that. I love that song."

"I love it too," I told her. "It wasn't until I heard Beverly Sills sing it years ago on TV that I realized it didn't always have to be done in pop or jazz style."

Then Richard Shelton walked in the door, just in time for some fresh, fragrant coffee. He bet me it wasn't going to rain; this wasn't the season. He lost. I told him about "All the Things You Are." He was tickled and rightfully proud of Lois's voice. She'd been starring in Southwestern musical productions for years. I'd already met Richard in California and had long admired his work. Lois was the one who'd guided me patiently to the Tucson Airport and picked me up there after I'd booked myself into Phoenix. At the University of Arizona Poetry Center, which she quietly directed, I'd seen smart photographic portraits of writers she'd taken.

Beyond that, I'd had no idea of all the things she was.

Late that night, peaceful in my campus bed, a visiting writer and guest of the University, I lay thinking about all the things we truly are; thinking about the vast, crystalline silence of the desert and how it restively nurtures reflection. While crickets chirped in the bathroom at Poetry House and an occasional unconcerned lizard zipped across the floor of my snug bedroom, I lay remembering "Bird of Paradise," Charlie Parker's version of "All the Things You Are" and the chord it had set quivering in me years and years ago. For nights and mornings on end, I'd never wanted those changes to change.

Whether I'd been thinking birds or flowers, the paradise Parker had pulled me into, I realized in Arizona, was all intact. It was all still there; omnipresent in a finely muted region of spirit, the basis for everything, where nothing ever changes or moves or comes or goes or withers or blooms. It was all too divinely simple for my rambling, self-centered human mind to grasp just then, yet the meaning of it all, like my scrambling at the piano to keep pace with Lois Shelton's vocalizing, pianist that I wasn't, was beginning to ring clear all the same. Like everyone else, I vaguely identified with all things, and it was only my awareness of this that needed sharpening. There existed a part of me that already knew all there was to know; it was only a matter of connecting with it.

That night, just before shifting from wakefulness to the middle of dream, I slipped into that delectable state where the thinker who's still busy calling out chord changes makes blissful peace with the player who's already playing. As I lay in this state, there appeared before me, in effortless recall, that portion of wall in the next room, where guests had taken turns scrawling a highly specialized graffiti, these words in flawless English of the Russian poet Yevgeny Yevtushenko:

> I bless all those unblessed by God;
> Those with shoes and those unshod.

The surprise of all surprises, however, came when I happened upon a note I'd written in 1977 titled *ALL THE THINGS YOU ARE*. It read as follows: *The mind-blessed bend of a rainstorm aiming in a hurting direction, it's almost as if we were all fake piano players smoothing out mistakes with a false, facile flourish. You are the wash of a wave over stones left wet. You are the way wheat looks after it's been mauled. You are another afternoon.*

Tell me about promised kisses, springtime, September, the desert, lightning storms, rain, the power of poetry and song and why the lonely winter seems long. Slowly tell me all the things you are, we are, I am—and sing it.

Al Young

A native of Ocean Springs, Mississippi, Al Young also grew up in Michigan and attended college in Ann Arbor. At age 21, he visited the San Francisco Bay Area, fell in love with it and has been based there ever since. A prolific writer, he has published over a dozen books since the appearance of his first book of poems, *Dancing* in 1969, and his first novel, *Snakes* in 1970. He has also written numerous articles, essays, LP liner notes and screenplays for various publications, companies, and people, including: *Rolling Stone, Essence, The New York Times, Harper's, Parabola, Paris Review, TriQuarterly, Evergreen,* Warner Bros., Concord Jazz, Universal Studios, Joseph Strick, The Robert Stigwood Organization, Sidney Poitier, Bill Cosby and Richard Pryor. With poet-novelist Ishmael Reed, Young edits *Quilt,* an international journal devoted to multicultural writing. His work has been translated into Spanish, French, German, Italian, Norwegian, Japanese, Polish and Chinese. Honors include the Wallace E. Stegner Writing Fellowship, the Joseph Henry Jackson Award, a Guggenheim Fellowship, a National Endowment for the Arts Fellowship, the Pushcart Prize, a Fulbright Fellowship, the Before Columbus Foundation American Book Award, and the Key to the City of Detroit. He has held teaching posts at many colleges and universities and at the present moment is a visiting professor at the Merrill College Field Studies Program at the University of California at Santa Cruz.